TIME ZONES

THIRD EDITION

DAVID BOHLKE

JENNIFER WILKIN

NATIONAL GEOGRAPHIC
LEARNING

Australia · Brazil · Mexico · Singapore · United Kingdom · United States

National Geographic Learning,
a Cengage Company

Time Zones 3 Third Edition

David Bohlke and Jennifer Wilkin

Publisher: Andrew Robinson

Managing Editor: Derek Mackrell

Associate Development Editor: Don Clyde Bhasy

Director of Global Marketing: Ian Martin

Senior Product Marketing Manager: Anders Bylund

Heads of Regional Marketing:
    Charlotte Ellis (Europe, Middle East and Africa)
    Kiel Hamm (Asia)
    Irina Pereyra (Latin America)

Senior Production Controller: Tan Jin Hock

Associate Media Researcher: Jeffrey Millies

Senior Designer: Lisa Trager

Operations Support: Rebecca G. Barbush,
    Hayley Chwazik-Gee

Manufacturing Planner: Mary Beth Hennebury

Composition: Symmetry Creative Productions, Inc.

For permission to use material from this text or product,
submit all requests online at **cengage.com/permissions**
Further permissions questions can be emailed to
permissionrequest@cengage.com

Student's Book with Online Practice
ISBN-13: 978-0-357-42170-3

Student's Book
ISBN-13: 978-0-357-41893-2

National Geographic Learning
200 Pier 4 Boulevard
Boston, MA 02210
USA

Locate your local office at **international.cengage.com/region**

Visit National Geographic Learning online at **ELTNGL.com**
Visit our corporate website at **www.cengage.com**

Printed in Mexico
Print Number: 01   Print Year: 2020

CONTENTS

SCOPE AND SEQUENCE

UNIT	FUNCTIONS	GRAMMAR	VOCABULARY	PRONUNCIATION	READ, WRITE, & WATCH
1 I'D LIKE TO BE A PILOT					PAGE 6
	Talking about jobs and goals Giving career advice **Real English:** *You know …*	**Using *want* and *would like*:** *What kind of job do you want?* *What kind of job would you like?* *I want a job that allows me to …* *I'd like a job that involves …* *I want to be a vet.* *I'd like to work as a firefighter.*	Jobs Job qualities Suffix: *-ous*	Weak forms of *that*	**Reading:** Extreme Jobs **Writing:** Email **Video:** Volcano Explorers
2 WHICH ONE IS BRUNO?					PAGE 18
	Identifying and describing people **Real English:** *Hang on!*	**Using *the one who*:** *Which one is Tyler?* *He's the one who's watching TV.* **Adjectives:** *What's she like?* *She's a little shy.* *She's really funny.*	Personality adjectives Compound adjectives	Syllable stress	**Reading:** Unsung Heroes **Writing:** Blog post **Video:** The Tables
3 WE HAVE TO REDUCE TRASH!					PAGE 30
	Talking about rules Discussing plastic waste **Real English:** *Of course!*	**Using language for rules:** *You have to bring your own bag.* *You can't throw that here.* *You're allowed to put plastic in this bin.*	Rules Plastic pollution Prefix: *re-* Suffix: *-able*	Reduction of *has to* and *have to*	**Reading:** 6 Things You Can Do About Plastic **Writing:** Social media post **Video:** Fixing the Plastic Problem
4 HOW DO SLOTHS MOVE?					PAGE 42
	Describing characteristics and behavior Talking about animals **Real English:** *Yuck!*	**Adjectives and adverbs:** *Sloths are slow.* *Sloths move slowly.* *Dolphins are good swimmers.* *Dolphins swim well.*	Animals Animal characteristics Phrasal verbs with *come*	Unstressed schwa syllables	**Reading:** Can Animals Be Nice? **Writing:** Online ad **Video:** Amazing Rats
5 I'M MEETING FRIENDS LATER					PAGE 54
	Discussing future events and plans **Real English:** *I'm afraid …*	**Simple present:** *The train arrives tomorrow morning.* *What time does the party start?* **Present progressive:** *I'm meeting friends on Saturday.* *What are you doing in the evening?*	Common activities Suffixes: *-ed* and *-ing*	Stress in compound nouns	**Reading:** Sit with Us **Writing:** Email **Video:** The Boiling River
6 WHAT WILL EARTH BE LIKE IN THE FUTURE?					PAGE 66
	Making predictions Describing changes **Real English:** *Are you serious?*	**Using *will* and *won't*:** *It will be hotter in the future.* *There won't be enough food.* **Using *more, less,* and *fewer*:** *There'll be more people.* *There'll be less farmland.* *There'll be fewer polar bears.*	Climate change The environment Suffix: *-y*	Reduction of *will*	**Reading:** On Thin Ice **Writing:** Short paragraph **Video:** Renewable Energy

1

I'D LIKE TO BE A PILOT

PREVIEW

A   🎧 1.1 **Listen.** Circle the kind of job each student wants.

1 Caitlyn wants a job that's **easy / fun**.   ○   ○   accountant

2 Danny wants a job that allows him to **be creative / travel**.   ○   ○   doctor

3 Yumiko wants a job that's **exciting / rewarding**.   ○   ○   pilot

4 Miguel wants a job that involves working with **animals / children**. ○   ○   singer

5 Sara wants a job that **challenges her / pays well**.   ○   ○   vet

An American pilot in an F-16 fighter jet

B 🎧 1.2 **Guess.** Match the students with the jobs. Then listen and check your answers.

C **Work with a partner.** What other jobs match the descriptions in **A**?

What other jobs are fun? | I know. An actor!

UNIT GOALS

• learn about jobs and career choices

• use language for talking about goals

• find out about interesting and extreme jobs

LANGUAGE FOCUS

A 🎧 **1.3 Listen and read.** What kind of job would Nadine like to have someday? Then repeat the conversation and replace the words in **bold**.

> **REAL ENGLISH** You know . . .

Nadine: Look at this app. You enter information, and it recommends a job for you.

Maya: Really? What kind of information?

Nadine: Well, I said I want a job that allows me to work **with computers**. I also said that I'm good with details. (**with numbers** / **in an office**)

Maya: So what job did it **recommend**? (**suggest** / **say was good for you**)

Nadine: An accountant. But I don't want to work as an accountant. It **sounds a little boring**. (**doesn't sound fun** / **doesn't interest me**)

Maya: What **would you like to do**? (**do you want to do** / **job would you prefer**)

Nadine: You know, I really want to work as an app developer. I'd like to create apps, but apps that are better than this one!

B 🎧 **1.4 Look at the chart.** Circle the correct words to complete the sentences below.

TALKING ABOUT CAREER GOALS (USING *WANT* AND *WOULD LIKE*)	
What kind of job **do** you **want**? What kind of job **would** you **like**?	I **want** a job **that** pays a lot of money. I**'d like** a job **that allows** me **to** travel. I**'d like** a job **that involves** working with animals.
What **do** you **want to be** someday? What **would** you **like to do** someday?	I **want to be** a vet. I**'d like to be** a flight attendant. I**'d love to** work as an app developer.

1 *Want* and *would like* mean **the same thing** / **different things**.

2 After *want* and *would like,* we use **to + base verb** / **verb + ing**.

3 After *that allows me*, we use **to + base verb** / **verb + ing**.

4 After *that involves*, we use **to + base verb** / **verb + ing**.

C **Complete the sentences.** Use the correct form of the words and phrases in the box.

> travel ~~be creative~~ work with animals
> dangerous pay well work with technology

1 Maria would like to be a designer because she wants a job that allows her to _be creative_ .

2 Juan doesn't want to be a police officer. He doesn't want a job that's _____ .

3 Mia and Joe want to work as bankers because they want jobs that _____ .

4 I want to work on a cruise ship because I want a job that allows me to _____ .

5 Salma wants to develop software. She'd like a job that involves _____ .

6 I'd like to be a vet. I'd like a job that allows me to _____ .

D 🎧 **1.5 Complete the conversation.** Circle the correct words. Then listen and check.

Misha: This job fair looks great! What kind of job ¹ **do / would** you like to have?

Carl: Hmm. I think I'd ² **like / likes** a job that ³ **allow / allows** me to travel.

Misha: Like a flight attendant? They travel all the time!

Carl: No, I ⁴ **want / would** to do something that's more exciting.

Misha: Why don't you work ⁵ **as / with** a pilot?

Carl: I'm not sure …

Misha: Hmm. So what ⁶ **want / would** you like to do?

Carl: I don't know. I think I don't want a job. I'd just ⁷ **like / want** to travel!

E **Work in groups.** Think of a job. Other students take turns asking yes/no questions to try to guess the job.

Is it a job that pays well?

I think so.

Is it a job that's dangerous?

A zookeeper looks after a baby tiger.

BEST JOB *EVER*

Jessica Cramp is part of a submarine team working in the Galápagos Islands.

A ▶ **1.1** **Watch the video.** Circle the correct answers.

1 Jessica works as **an underwater photographer** / **a marine biologist**.

2 Jessica says her job allows her to **visit many countries** / **study many animals**.

3 Jessica thinks her team is the world's **youngest** / **only** all-woman submarine team.

B ▶ **1.1** **Watch again.** Match the two parts of the sentences.

1 They are in a submarine	○	○ that she loves.
2 They are learning about an area	○	○ that can go very deep.
3 Jessica has a job	○	○ that they are trying to protect.

DO YOU KNOW?

Which of these is the most popular dream job of children in the USA?
a actor
b teacher
c scientist

C **Complete the passage about the Galápagos Islands.** Use the words in the box.

| far | underwater | unique | west |

The Galápagos Islands are in the Pacific Ocean, ¹ _____ of Ecuador. But what makes these islands special? For starters, they're ² _____ from the mainland—about 1,000 kilometers away. This makes the nature there ³ _____—there are animals that aren't found anywhere else, like its giant tortoises, and its iguanas that swim ⁴ _____ .

D CRITICAL THINKING Interpreting **Talk with a partner.** Jessica says that she feels like "a real explorer." What do you think she means?

PROJECT Go online and find a job that interests you. What skills, education, and experience do you need?

PRONUNCIATION weak forms of *that*

🎧 1.6 **Listen to the weak form of *that* in sentence 1.** Then underline the weak form of *that* when it appears in the other sentences. Listen again and repeat the sentences.

1 Jessica has a job that she finds exciting.
2 She learns about animals that are amazing.
3 That fish is called a *mola mola*.
4 There's only one animal that swims like that.

COMMUNICATION

A **Look at the chart.** Read the interview questions. Add four ideas of your own.

Do you want a job that … ?	
☐ involves working with animals	☐ has regular hours
☐ is interesting and rewarding	☐ challenges you
☐ allows you to work outside	☐ pays a lot of money
☐	☐
☐	☐

B **Interview a partner.** What kind of job does your partner want? Ask questions and check (✓) the items in **A**. Then give some career advice.

Do you want a job that involves working with animals?

Yes, I think I'd like that.

READING

A Skim the article. What does *extreme* mean? Who do you think has the more extreme job, and why?

B Scan the article. Match the words to their meaning.

1 astronaut ○　○ a very dry place with little rain
2 desert ○　○ types of medicine
3 poison ○　○ a person who travels to space
4 drugs ○　○ something that harms you if it enters your body

C Scan the article. Underline all the jobs. There are five.

Wang Yaping was the second woman from China to travel to space.

EXTREME JOBS

A. 🎧 1.7 **Wang Yaping** has a job that allows her to travel—all the way to space. Wang is an astronaut. In 2013, she became the second Chinese woman to travel to space. She is also famous for a physics class that she televised from space to more than 60 million people.

B Wang **trained** very hard for many years to become an astronaut. The toughest part was desert training. Wearing a spacesuit and carrying heavy **equipment**, she walked several kilometers through the hot and sandy desert. "Sometimes it was so windy and dusty," she says, "that we couldn't see each other even [though we] were just a few meters away."

C Wang loves her job. She remembers watching the first Chinese astronaut go into space. "I was so **proud** and also very excited. But as I watched it, it occurred to me: We have male pilots and female pilots. And then a male astronaut. When will there be a female astronaut? And today, it's me becoming one of the first few."

D **Zoltan Takacs** is a snake **researcher**. He first became interested in snakes when he was a teacher in Budapest, Hungary. Today, snakes are his career. He travels to many different countries around the world to study all kinds of dangerous snakes.

E Takacs studies snake venom—the poison a snake produces to kill other animals. He hopes his research will help him discover new life-saving drugs. There are over 100,000 types of venomous animals in the world. "Imagine how many **potential** medications you could find," he says.

F Being a snake researcher allows Takacs to travel to many beautiful and **remote** places. But it is also dangerous. He has been bitten by venomous snakes six times, but has learned to be careful. "Explorers have to know their limits," he says. "Then we can push those limits further."

Zoltan Takacs travels the world in search of deadly snakes.

COMPREHENSION

A Answer the questions about *Extreme Jobs*.

1 `DETAIL` Which statement about Wang is true?

   a She had an accident in space.

   b She taught a physics class from space.

   c She is the first Chinese woman to travel to space.

2 `DETAIL` What did Wang do to become an astronaut?

   a She trained in a tough environment.

   b She taught physics.

   c She lived by herself for several months.

3 `PURPOSE` What is the purpose of paragraph C?

   a to describe China's first space mission

   b to explain why Wang wanted to become an astronaut

   c to show that being an astronaut is difficult

4 `COHESION` What is the best place for this sentence in paragraph E?

"He also studies the venom of other animals."

   a after the first sentence   **b** after the third sentence   **c** after the last sentence

5 `VOCABULARY` The phrase "push those limits further" (paragraph F) is closest in meaning to _____ .

   a do even greater things

   b stop before something bad happens

   c make other people do things for you

IDIOM

An example of a person with a "nine-to-five" job is _____ .
a an astronaut
b an accountant
c a dancer

B Complete the Venn diagram. Write the letters (a–f).

   a has a job that's exciting
   b is trying to save lives
   c used technology to teach students
   d has a job that lets him/her travel
   e trained in a desert
   f works with dangerous animals

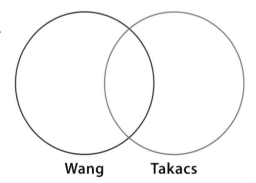

Wang   Takacs

C `CRITICAL THINKING Analyzing` Talk with a partner. Which job from the reading did you say was more extreme? Do you still feel that way? Why or why not?

VOCABULARY

A **Find these words in the article.** Then complete the definitions.

> train   equipment   proud   researcher   potential   remote

1 If a solution is possible, it's a(n) _____ solution.

2 A person who studies something to find out more is a(n) _____ .

3 To get better at something, you have to _____ .

4 A place that is far away from everything is _____ .

5 A person who feels good about something they did is _____ .

6 _____ refers to the set of items you need to do an activity.

B **Read the information below.** Then complete the sentences using the *-ous* form of the words in the box.

> The suffix *-ous* means "full of" or "having the qualities of." It can turn some nouns into adjectives.
>
> *venom* → *venomous*
>
> a *venomous* snake: one that has venom

A firefighter from the US

> adventure   danger   fame   poison

1 It's easy for firefighters to get hurt. It's a(n) _____ job.

2 You should go to a hospital if you drink something _____ .

3 After Wang's first trip to space, she became _____ .

4 He likes going to remote places. He's a(n) _____ traveler.

WRITING

A **Read the email to a guidance counselor.**

B **What kind of job would you like?** Make notes.

C **Write an email to a guidance counselor.** Ask for career advice. Describe the type of job you would like.

New message

To

Subject

Dear Ms. Rodriguez,

My name is Vivian. I would like some help choosing a job. I really enjoy helping people. I'd like a job that's rewarding and that involves …

Send

VOLCANO EXPLORERS

Before You Watch

Match the words to their meaning.

1 lava   ○   ○ a flying machine that you control from the ground
2 crater   ○   ○ the hot, red liquid that comes out of volcanoes
3 drone   ○   ○ the opening at the top of a volcano

While You Watch

A ▶ 1.2 **Watch the video.** Which sentence best describes the main idea?

  a A filmmaker makes a movie about a scientist and a volcano.

  b A scientist uses drones to collect rocks from the mouth of a volcano.

  c Two people with different jobs work together in a new and exciting way.

B ▶ 1.2 **Watch again.** Circle **T** for True or **F** for False.

  1 Sam is making a 3D model of the volcano.   **T**   **F**

  2 Sometimes, drones get destroyed by the volcano.   **T**   **F**

  3 There are lifeforms living inside the volcano's lava. **T**   **F**

  4 Jeffrey wants to learn how life first began on Earth. **T**   **F**

C **Check (✓) the correct options.** How does Sam's work
help Jeffrey? Jeffrey can use Sam's footage to:

  ☐ find out where he collected a sample from.

  ☐ watch how life forms in the rocks.

  ☐ study the different layers of the volcano.

After You Watch

Talk with a partner. What are some other
jobs that would benefit from drones?

A Complete the sentences. Use the names of jobs found in this unit.

1 _Firefighters_ have jobs that are dangerous.

2 _____ care for injured animals.

3 _____ and flight _____ work on airplanes.

4 _____ treat sick people.

5 App _____ create programs for cell phones.

6 _____ are people who work in space.

7 _____ use cameras to make movies.

8 Marine _____ study life in the ocean.

B Complete the sentences. Circle the correct words.

1 I want a job that **paying** / **pays** well.

2 He'd **like** / **likes** to work with animals.

3 I want a job that allows me **traveling** / **to travel**.

4 She wants to work **as** / **to** a flight attendant.

5 I have a job that involves **working** / **to work** with technology.

6 What kind of job **do** / **would** you like to have someday?

C Complete the sentences. Use words from the box with *-ous*.

adventure	danger	fame	poison

1 Working with snakes is _____.

2 Albert Einstein was a(n) _____ scientist.

3 Don't breathe in that gas. It's _____.

4 Only _____ people can work in extreme jobs.

SELF CHECK   Now I can …

☐ talk about jobs and career choices

☐ use language for talking about goals

☐ discuss interesting and extreme jobs

2

WHICH ONE IS BRUNO?

PREVIEW

A 🎧 2.1 **Listen.** Cassie is describing the people in the photo. Match the names and the descriptions.

1	Miguel ⚪	⚪ laughing at a joke	⚪	⚪ fun to be around
2	Veronica ⚪	⚪ wearing a yellow sweater	⚪	⚪ really helpful
3	Christina ⚪	⚪ listening to music	⚪	⚪ pretty easygoing
4	Bruno ⚪	⚪ walking behind Miguel	⚪	⚪ kind of quiet

B 🎧 2.1 **Listen again.** What is each person like? Match them to their personalities.

A group of friends in San Miguel de Allende, Mexico

PEOPLE AND PLACES

C **Work in groups.** Show photos of your friends and describe them.

> This is my friend Jason. He's really funny.

> This is Bianca. She's pretty outgoing and loves to joke.

UNIT GOALS

• learn how to talk about the people around us

• use language for identifying and describing people

• find out about heroes and inspirational people

LANGUAGE FOCUS

A 🎧 2.2 **Listen and read.** Who are Stig and Ming meeting at the airport? Then repeat the conversation and replace the words in **bold**.

> **REAL ENGLISH** Hang on!

Stig: Thanks for coming with me to **meet** my cousin Ursula. (**welcome / pick up**)

Ming: No problem, Stig. So, is Ursula the one who **texts you all the time**? (**calls you late at night / always sends you videos**)

Stig: No, that's my cousin Ingrid.

Ming: Oh, right. What's Ursula like?

Stig: Well, she's a lot like me. She's tall and stylish, and she's really **fun**. (**popular / outgoing**)

Ming: Ah. Is she the one who travels a lot?

Stig: Yeah, that's right.

Ming: Oh, **I think I see her** … Hi! My name's Ming. It's nice to meet you! (**that must be her / there she is**)

Stig: Hang on, Ming! That's not Ursula. *That's* Ursula!

B 🎧 2.3 **Look at the chart.** Circle the correct answers.

IDENTIFYING AND DESCRIBING PEOPLE (USING *THE ONE WHO* AND ADJECTIVES)		
Identifying people	**Which one** is Tyler?	He's **the one who** called yesterday. He's **the one (who's)** watching TV.
	Which ones are your cousins?	They're **the ones** by the door / in green T-shirts.
Describing personality	**What's** Miguel **like**?	He's a little shy / kind of quiet.
	What are your cousins **like**?	They're really outgoing / a lot of fun.

1 To ask about personality, we use *What **is** / **does** she like?*

2 We use *Which one* to **identify someone / ask about personality**.

3 In *He's the one who's [verb + ing]*, the word *who's* is **necessary / optional**.

C **Complete the sentences.** Use the words from the box.

> patient   chatty   dependable   shy   funny

1 Marissa is always talking to people. She's really _____ .

2 Amos doesn't feel comfortable around other people. He's pretty _____ .

3 Hee-jin is always there when her friends need her. She's so _____ .

4 Michael makes all of his friends laugh. He's very _____ .

5 Patricia never gets upset when her friends are late. She's extremely _____ .

D 🎧 **2.4** **Join the sentences.** Then listen and check. Find the people in the photo below.

1 That's Craig. He always sits in the front row.
   Craig is the one who _____ .

2 Her name is Suzy. She's sitting next to Craig.
   _____ .

3 Those two are Debbie and Sonia. They always study together.
   _____ .

4 That's Evelyn. She wearing a yellow sweater.
   _____ .

E **Work with a partner. Student A:** Go to page 150. **Student B:** Go to page 152.
You are going to identify people at a party.

A PHOTOGRAPHER'S JOURNEY

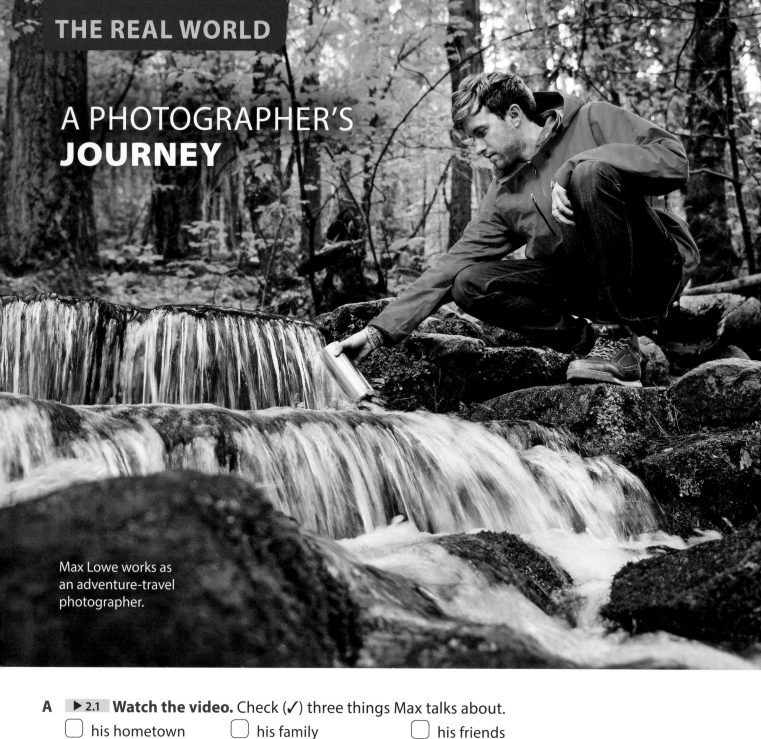

Max Lowe works as an adventure-travel photographer.

A ▶ 2.1 **Watch the video.** Check (✓) three things Max talks about.

☐ his hometown ☐ his family ☐ his friends

☐ his school life ☐ his future plans ☐ his heroes

B ▶ 2.1 **Watch the video.** Circle the correct answers.

1 Long ago, Max wanted to be **an explorer** / **a pilot**.

2 In high school, he wanted to become a **journalist** / **photographer**.

3 His **parents** / **teacher** gave him his first digital camera.

4 Max's **father** / **mother** is the one who introduced him to the outdoors.

C **Complete the passage.** Use the words in the box.

> good   inspires   needs   strong   supports

When we hear the word "hero," we often think of men or women who are ¹ _____ enough to punch through walls, or who can fly. In the real world, heroes are usually more down to earth. A hero is someone who ² _____ us to be better. Some heroes are really ³ _____ at something, while others put the ⁴ _____ of others first. A hero can even be someone who's always there for you, and who ⁵ _____ you when you need a helping hand. So who are your heroes?

DO YOU KNOW?

In ancient Greece, the word *hero* meant "someone who _____."
a fights
b rescues
c protects

D [CRITICAL THINKING Reflecting] **Do you have any heroes?** What makes them special?

> **PROJECT Interview three people outside of class.** Find out who their heroes are, and why.

PRONUNCIATION syllable stress

🎧 2.5 **Listen.** Underline the stressed syllable. Then listen again and repeat the words.

1 photography	**3** important	**5** introduce
2 hero	**4** inspire	**6** supportive

COMMUNICATION

A **Play a guessing game.** Write four things about yourself on four pieces of paper. Fold them in half. Don't show anyone!

I'm good at singing.

I'm shy around new people.

My favorite superhero is Iron Man.

I take piano lessons.

B **Work in a group.** Put the pieces of paper on a table. Then take turns choosing pieces and guessing who wrote each one. When you guess correctly, keep the paper.

I think Kenji is the one who takes piano lessons.

Sorry, it's not me.

READING

A **Read the title.** What do you think an unsung hero is?
a a hero who makes a mistake
b a hero who isn't famous
c a hero who dislikes being a hero

B **Scan the text.** Underline the names of the three unsung heroes.

C **Skim the text.** Label the paragraphs with these headings.
a Reinventing the Wheel
b The Other Steve
c The Third Man

Michael Collins was the pilot of the famous Apollo 11 spacecraft.

UNSUNG *HEROES*

🎧 **2.6** Unsung heroes are people who **achieve** something important, but who are not known for it. Here are three such people.

1 _____

5　When Neil Armstrong and Buzz Aldrin flew to the moon in 1969, a third astronaut went with them. Michael Collins was the "forgotten astronaut"—the pilot who flew the Apollo 11 spacecraft into space. After Armstrong and Aldrin landed on the moon, Collins flew
10　around it several times until they were ready to leave. He was **completely** alone and often out of radio contact. But he wasn't afraid. When it was time to leave, Collins came through. He reconnected with the moon lander and returned everyone to Earth as heroes.

15　**2** _____

When people think of the tech **giant** Apple, they usually think of Steve Jobs. Not many people think about his partner, Steve Wozniak. But both Jobs and Wozniak started the company that **transformed** the
20　computer industry. Steve Jobs took care of the business side, but Wozniak's role was just as important. He was the one who built Apple's first computer. He also **designed** the next one. And the one after that! Jobs became the famous face of Apple. But many who know
25　the company's history believe that the shy and lesser-known Steve was the true visionary.

3 _____

Go to any train station or airport and there are hundreds of people wheeling their luggage. But things
30　weren't always this way. In the 1970s, people had to carry their heavy suitcases—back then, suitcases didn't have wheels! Bernard Sadow was the one who changed all that. He was at an airport when he saw a worker pushing a heavy machine around using a platform with
35　wheels. He said to his wife, "That's what we need on luggage." He went home and **attached** wheels to a suitcase, changing the history of travel forever.

COMPREHENSION

A Answer the questions about *Unsung Heroes.*

IDIOM

If you go "from zero to hero," _____.
a you meet your hero
b your situation becomes more difficult
c things improve for you greatly

1 **MAIN IDEA** The passage is about people who _____.

   a came close to succeeding

   b succeeded at their jobs

   c didn't try hard enough

2 **DETAIL** What is NOT true about Michael Collins?

   a He was a pilot.   b He was an astronaut.   c He walked on the moon.

3 **DETAIL** Both Steve Jobs and Steve Wozniak _____.

   a built Apple's first computer   b started Apple together   c were the faces of Apple

4 **VOCABULARY** A *visionary* (line 26) is someone who _____.

   a comes up with a great idea

   b becomes the face of a company

   c manages a business well

5 **REFERENCE** In line 35, *That* refers to _____.

   a platforms   b wheels   c machines

B Match the sentences to the people. Write **M** (Michael Collins), **S** (Steve Wozniak), or **B** (Bernard Sadow).

_____ He invented something modern and high tech.

_____ He invented something simple but very useful.

_____ He went somewhere dangerous.

_____ His idea came after a moment of inspiration.

_____ He was responsible for other people's lives.

C CRITICAL THINKING Ranking Talk with a partner. Whose achievement made the biggest difference? Rank them from most (1) to least (3) for each category. Then discuss as a class.

	Collins	Wozniak	Sadow
the most well known			
the most inspiring			
changed society for the better			
affected you the most personally			

VOCABULARY

A **Find these words in the article.** Then complete the sentences.

> achieved   completely   giant   transformed   designed   attached

1 The internet _____ the way we look for information.

2 He _____ wheels to the chair using screws.

3 She's really famous. She's a(n) _____ in the world of jazz music.

4 I have no idea where I am. I'm _____ lost.

5 After many years of trying, I finally _____ my goals.

6 They _____ the website to be simple and easy to use.

B **Read the information below.** Then complete the sentences using the words in the box. Use a hyphen when necessary.

> Sometimes, two words can be joined to create a compound adjective.
>   *lesser-known*: not as famous
> We only hyphenate these expressions when they appear before a noun:
>   With hyphen: *Wozniak is the lesser-known Steve.*
>   Without hyphen: *Compared to Steve Jobs, Wozniak is lesser known.*

> well known   much needed   well written   last minute

1 The book is _____ . It's interesting from start to finish.

2 That was a _____ vacation. I feel a lot better now.

3 She completed her assignment at the very _____ .

4 He's not famous here, but he's a(n) _____ actor in his home town.

WRITING

A **Read the blog post.** Look at the photo.

B **Who is your hero?** Find a photo of that person and write notes about what makes them special.

C **Write a blog post.** Describe your hero and why you admire them.

HOME   ABOUT US   **BLOG**   FAQ   CONTACT US

MY HERO

My grandmother is my hero. She is hardworking and serious, but she's also outgoing and funny. She's the one who …

THE *TABLES*

Before You Watch

Talk with a partner. What do you know about New York City? Circle the correct answers.

1 New York City is the **capital of** / **largest city in** the United States.

2 About **10** / **40** percent of New Yorkers are from other countries.

3 The biggest park in New York City is **Bryant Park** / **Central Park**.

While You Watch

A ▶ 2.2 **Watch the video.** Circle the correct answers. The video talks about:

1 **the history of Bryant Park**	OR	**the regulars at Bryant Park**
2 **the rules of ping pong**	OR	**the personalities of the players**
3 **who built the tables**	OR	**where the players come from**

B ▶ 2.2 **Watch again.** Pay attention to the names. Match the parts of the sentences.

1 Darren is the one who ○ ○ plays with a wooden block.
2 Tyrone is the one who ○ ○ is always there.
3 Wally is the one who ○ ○ attacks every high ball.
4 Sergio is the one who ○ ○ laughs and jokes a lot.
5 Gregory is the one who ○ ○ plays professionally for the US.

C **Talk with a partner.** What do these expressions mean? Circle the correct answer.

1 Darren's a *real open guy*. He's **easy to talk to** / **never busy**.

2 Gregory's *the rock of the park*. He's **always serious** / **reliable**.

3 Wally is an *undercover guy*. He **doesn't tell people his job** / **works as a detective**.

After You Watch

Talk with a partner. How do people in your city meet and bond? What would you build to help people meet and make friends?

REVIEW

A Replace the bold words. Use a word that has a similar meaning.

> shy   easygoing   dependable   outgoing

1 Omar's very **quiet** when he meets new people. _____

2 Lanya's pretty **relaxed**. She won't mind that you're late. _____

3 Paula is really **friendly**. She loves people and parties. _____

4 You can always count on Ben. He's super **reliable**! _____

B Complete the sentences. Write the correct words.

> what's   which   who's   with

1 **A:** _____ one is Tyler?

   B: He's the one _____ the long hair.

2 **C:** _____ Anton like?

   D: He's pretty quiet, but sometimes he's funny.

3 **E:** Is that Paulita?

   F: No, Paulita's the one _____ standing by the door.

C Complete the sentences. Add hyphens when needed.

> well known   much needed   well written   last minute

1 He didn't plan to go. It was a _____ decision.

3 The Beatles were a _____ band from the UK.

3 This paragraph is bad, but the next one is _____.

4 The school received _____ money for new equipment.

Ping pong at Bryant Park

SELF CHECK   Now I can …

☐ talk about the people around me

☐ use language for identifying and describing people

☐ discuss heroes and inspirational people

3

WE HAVE TO REDUCE TRASH!

PREVIEW

A 🎧 3.1 **Listen to a talk.** Circle the correct answers.

1 The main problem with plastic is that it **is poisonous** / **doesn't go away**.

2 The most important rule is to **recycle more** / **use less** plastic.

3 The speaker asks us to **think more about** / **recycle all of** the plastic we use.

B 🎧 3.1 **Listen again.** Match the rules and the examples.

1 reduce ○   ○ Separate plastic items. Don't throw them away.

2 reuse ○   ○ Use paper or cloth bags, not plastic ones.

3 recycle ○   ○ Turn a soda bottle into a pencil holder.

A jellyfish swims in an ocean littered with plastic waste.

THE NATURAL WORLD

- learn about the plastic problem
- use language for talking about rules
- find out ways you can help reduce plastic waste

C Work with a partner. What else do you know about the problem of trash? What are some things people can do to help?

> People can stop buying bottled water.

> Right! And they can carry reusable straws.

LANGUAGE FOCUS

A 🎧 **3.2** **Listen and read.** What two things does Ming do to avoid using plastic? Then repeat the conversation and replace the words in **bold**.

> **REAL ENGLISH** Of course!

Stig: Hey, you brought your own bag!

Ming: Of course! I always carry my own bag.

Stig: That's a **good** idea. You have to pay for plastic bags now. (**smart** / **clever**)

Maya: I think that's great! Single-use plastics create so much **waste**. (**trash** / **garbage**)

Stig: They're difficult to avoid, though. Every time you buy a drink, you **need** a plastic straw. (**have to use** / **get**)

Maya: That's not really true. Many places use eco-friendly straws—ones you can recycle.

Ming: And I have a reusable straw that I carry **all the time**. (**around** / **everywhere**)

Maya: In some places, stores aren't allowed to give out plastic straws anymore. I hope the idea catches on!

B 🎧 **3.3** **Look at the chart.** Match the correct sentences together.

TALKING ABOUT RULES (USING *HAVE TO*, *ALLOWED TO*, AND *CAN*)	
You **have to** bring your own bags to this store.	
He isn't **allowed to** put that in this bin.	
She **can** leave her plastic waste here.	
Do I **have to** bring my own bag?	Yes, you **do**. / No, you **don't**.
Can I leave my trash here?	Yes, you **can**. / No, you **can't**.
Am I **allowed to** throw my trash here?	Yes, you **are**. / No, you**'re not**. / No, you **aren't**.

1 You **have to** do something.   ○   ○ It's OK to NOT do it.

2 You **can't** do something.   ○   ○ It's NOT OK to do it.

3 You **don't have to** do something. ○   ○ It's NOT OK to NOT do it.

C **Read the rules.** Rewrite them using *can't*, *have to*, or *not allowed to*.

1. You can't / aren't allowed to walk on the grass.
2. _____
3. _____
4. _____
5. _____
6. _____

1. Don't walk on the grass.
2. Stay on the path.
3. Don't feed the animals.
4. Don't play loud music.
5. Recycle your bottles.
6. Walk your bike.

D 🎧 3.4 **Complete the conversations.** Write the correct words. Listen and check.

1. **Adam:** _____ we _____ our bikes here? (**allowed to / park**)

   Joe: No. You _____ them in the parking lot. (**have to / leave**)

2. **Justin:** _____ I _____ my phone? (**have to / turn off**)

   Taylor: No. But you _____ on it. (**not talk**)

3. **Megan:** _____ I _____ the bike path for running? (**can / use**)

   Walt: You _____ on it, but it's really for bikes. (**allowed to / run**)

4. **Jenny:** _____ she _____ a ticket at the airport? (**have to / buy**)

   Carlos: No, she _____. She can buy one online. (**not**)

5. **Fiona:** _____ we _____ in groups? (**allowed to / work**)

   Cindy: Yes, we are. We _____ alone. (**not have to / work**)

E **Think about the rules in your school, home, or another place.** Write three true and three false rules. Then share them in a group. Can the others guess the false rules?

You're not allowed to drink coffee in the library.

I think that's true.

TRAVELING WITHOUT SINGLE-USE PLASTIC

People often throw away plastic items while traveling, such as this cotton swab.

A **Talk with a partner.** What are single-use plastics? Can you name some examples?

B ▶ **3.1** **Watch the video.** Travel writer Marie McGrory lists some of the items she brought to Belize. Match the pictures and the words.

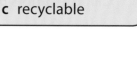

| a | b | c | d | e | f |

1 reusable utensils _____	**2** soap _____	**3** water bottle _____
4 reusable straw _____	**5** shampoo _____	**6** reusable bag _____

C ▶ 3.1 **Watch again.** Match Marie's four tips (**1–4**) to the descriptions (**a–d**). Which tip do you think is the most useful?

    a It was great for storing food and carrying it around.
    b Most of the places she stayed in had purified water stations.
    c Get your ice cream in a cone so that you don't need a plastic cup.
    d A glass straw isn't helpful if you don't say, "No straw, please."

    1 You have to ask. _____   **3** Collapsible Tupperware is underrated. _____

    2 Research the water situation. _____   **4** You don't always need tools. _____

D CRITICAL THINKING Evaluation **Talk with a partner.** Which of Marie's items do you think makes the biggest difference? Which one makes the least difference?

PROJECT Spend a day using as few single-use plastic items as possible. Make a list of the single-use plastic items you avoided using. Share your list with the class.

PRONUNCIATION reduction of *has to* and *have to*

🎧 3.5 **Listen.** Complete the sentences. Then listen again and repeat the sentences.

1 _____ pay for plastic bags.
2 _____ put it in the correct bin.
3 _____ reduce plastic waste.
4 _____ bring a reusable straw.

COMMUNICATION

A **Work in groups.** Write a set of rules to help make your school more environmentally friendly.

What rules do we want for our school?

How about "You can't use plastic straws"?

B **Make signs.** Look at the examples below. Draw your own signs for the rules you wrote in **A**.

C **Share your signs with another group.** Can they guess the rules? Write down each other's rules using complete sentences.

READING

A Skim the article. Underline the six tips the article gives for using less plastic.

B Scan the first paragraph. Which word describes objects that break down quickly when left out in nature? Does this word describe plastics?

C Discuss. Do you already follow any of these tips?

The plastic that we throw away often ends up in giant landfills.

6 THINGS
YOU CAN DO ABOUT
PLASTIC

🎧 **3.6** Plastic pollution is a serious problem, and it's getting worse. Because plastics aren't biodegradable, they'll stay in our oceans for a long time. Scientists are trying to create plastics that break down quickly,
5 but the best solution for now is to use less plastic. Here are six tips that can help you:

Stop using plastic bags. Bring your own reusable ones to the store instead. Every year, people use a trillion plastic bags worldwide. In the United States
10 alone, people use 100 billion bags **annually**—that's almost one per person per day. But in Denmark, people use only four plastic bags a year! Denmark's **solution**? It passed the world's first bag **tax** in 1993.

Say "no" to straws. A study **revealed** that more than
15 8.3 billion plastic straws cover the world's beaches. Americans throw away 500 million plastic straws every day—about 1.5 per person.

Don't buy bottled water. Carry a refillable water bottle with you. Around the world, nearly a million
20 plastic bottles are thrown away every minute. The problem is so bad that in some places like Bundanoon, Australia, stores aren't allowed to sell bottled water anymore.

Avoid plastic packaging. Most of the things we buy
25 come in plastic packaging. It's everywhere, and some countries like France are trying to **ban** it. But there are things you can do, too: buy bar soap instead of liquid soap; buy things in bulk; and avoid fruit or vegetables packed in plastic.

30 **Recycle what you can**. In 2018, the world recycled only 18 percent of its plastic. Europe recycled about 30 percent, and China recycled 25 percent. But the US only recycled 9 percent—a drop in the bucket.

Don't litter. 73 percent of the litter found on the
35 world's beaches is plastic. The most common types of plastic litter? Cigarette butts, bottles and bottle caps, food packaging, and plastic bags.

COMPREHENSION

A Answer the questions about *6 Things You Can Do About Plastic*.

1 **PURPOSE** This passage is mainly for _____ .

   a scientists   **b** businesses   **c** ordinary people

2 **DETAIL** Which is NOT mentioned as a way to reduce the number of plastic bags?

   a put a tax on them   **b** stop making them   **c** switch to reusable bags

3 **REFERENCE** What does *it* in line 26 refer to?

   a plastic plates   **b** soap   **c** plastic packaging

4 **VOCABULARY** In line 28, buying something *in bulk* means buying _____ .

   a for other people   **b** a lot at once   **c** many different things

5 **DETAIL** According to the passage, which of the following should we NOT do?

   a Use liquid soap.   **b** Get a metal straw.   **c** Use a refillable bottle.

B Complete the sentences below. Write the name of a country or town.

1 _____ recycles less than 10% of its plastic.

2 _____ was the first country to make people pay a tax for plastic bags.

3 _____ makes it difficult for people to buy bottled water.

4 _____ is trying to end the use of plastic packaging.

5 _____ recycles a quarter of its plastic.

C CRITICAL THINKING Ranking How easy are the six tips to follow? Rank them from *easy* (1) to *difficult* (6). Then discuss with a partner.

_____ Stop using plastic bags.   _____ Avoid plastic packaging.

_____ Say "no" to straws.   _____ Recycle what you can.

_____ Don't buy bottled water.   _____ Don't litter.

This jar contains all the plastic waste that blogger Kathryn Kellogg produced in one year.

VOCABULARY

A **Find the words below in the article.** Then circle the correct answer.

1 Something that happens **annually** happens *often / once a year*.

2 A **solution** to a problem is how you *fix / understand* it.

3 Money from **tax** goes to *the government / a company*.

4 When a study **reveals** something, it is *new / common* information.

5 If you **avoid** something, you *try / try not* to use it.

6 You **ban** something if you want people to *stop / continue* doing it.

IDIOM

You use "a drop in the bucket" to refer to _____.
a a small amount of liquid
b a small part of a large total
c a large amount of something

B **Read the information below.** Then complete the sentences. Use the words in the box with *re-* and/or *-able*.

> Prefixes and suffixes can change the meaning of a word.
>
> The prefix *re-* means "again."   *redo*: do again
>
> The suffix *-able* means "you can do it."   *drinkable* water: water you can drink
>
> (*-able* is spelled *-ible* after some words)

| fill | notice | new | use |

1 My metal straw is _____, so I don't need plastic straws anymore.

2 You can _____ that bottle with water from the tap.

3 There was a small scratch on his car. It wasn't very _____.

4 _____ energy, like solar and wind energy, is better for the environment.

WRITING

A **Read the social media post.**

B **Think of a way to reduce plastic waste.** Look for useful information online and write notes.

C **Write a social media post.** Explain your idea and find a photo to go with your post.

LYP **LoveYourPlanet**
@ideashare.com
#reduce #plastic #waste

Plastic waste is a big problem, and we have to do something about it. My solution is a new law: stores aren't allowed to give plastic bags …

FIXING THE *PLASTIC PROBLEM*

Before You Watch

Talk with a partner. Look at the photo. These bowls are made from wheat. How are they better than plastic bowls?

While You Watch

A ▶ 3.2 **Watch the video.** What plastic items do you see? Name a few. Do you use any of them?

B ▶ 3.2 **Watch again.** Circle the correct answers.

1 Single-use plastics make up **10** / **40** percent of all plastic waste.

2 One natural solution to the plastic problem involves using **worms** / **birds**.

3 Scientists are using microbes to **get rid of plastic** / **create better plastics**.

4 Bioplastics are natural materials that **we can eat** / **break down quickly**.

C ▶ 3.2 **Who are the solutions meant for?** Write **E** (everyone), **S** (scientists), or **M** (manufacturers). Watch the video and check your answers.

1 Find ways to break down plastics that already exist. _____

2 Use fewer straws and plastic bags. _____

3 Make bioplastics using natural ingredients. _____

4 Recycle plastic. _____

5 Choose reusable alternatives. _____

6 Make products using rubber tree latex. _____

After You Watch

Talk with a partner. What do you think about the solutions discussed in the video? Can you think of other solutions?

REVIEW

A Read the words below. Are they part of the solution 🙂 or are they part of the plastic problem 🙁? Circle the correct face.

1 recycling   🙂 🙁

2 plastic bags   🙂 🙁

3 food packaging   🙂 🙁

4 reusable straws   🙂 🙁

5 biodegradable plastic   🙂 🙁

6 a ban on straws   🙂 🙁

7 a tax on bags   🙂 🙁

B Complete the sentences. Circle the correct words.

1 You **don't have to / can't** litter on the beach.

2 I **have to / am allowed to** be in class before nine tomorrow.

3 You **can't / have to** put plastic bags in the paper recycling bin.

4 Students **don't have to / aren't allowed to** go into the teachers' room.

C Complete the sentences. Use the words in the box with *re-* and/or *-able*.

fill	new	biodegrade	notice

1 Solar energy is a type of _____ energy.

2 Unlike plastic waste, food waste is _____.

3 The sign was far away and not very _____.

4 You can use that bottle again—it's _____.

SELF CHECK   Now I can …

☐ talk about the plastic problem

☐ use language for talking about rules

☐ discuss ways to reduce plastic waste

HOW DO SLOTHS *MOVE?*

A sloth climbs slowly up a tree.

PREVIEW

A 🎧 **4.1 Listen.** Where does the speaker say the animals are from?

1 sloths ○   ○ South Africa
2 bees ○   ○ the United States
3 owls ○   ○ the Amazon rainforest
4 dolphins ○   ○ all over the world

B 🎧 **4.1 Listen again.** Complete the sentences with the words in the box.

gracefully	hard	playfully
quickly	patiently	~~slowly~~

1 Sloths move ___slowly___ in the trees but _____ in the water.

2 Bees work very _____ to make honey.

3 Owls wait _____ for their food.

4 Dolphins swim _____. They jump _____ out of the water.

C **Talk with a partner.** Name animals that do these things.

move slowly	run quickly	sing loudly
swim gracefully	wait patiently	

> I think lions wait patiently.

> And they run quickly.

THE NATURAL WORLD

UNIT GOALS

• find out about animals and how they do things

• learn how to describe characteristics and behavior

• explore how animals can be kind to each other

43

LANGUAGE FOCUS

A 🎧 **4.2 Listen and read.** What does Nadine say about bats? Then repeat the conversation and replace the words in **bold**.

Nadine: Hey, Ming. Did you choose an animal for your project?

Ming: I did. We **have to** write about one that isn't well known, so I chose bats. (**need to / should**)

Nadine: Bats? Yuck! They're **disgusting**. (**so ugly / really scary**)

Ming: I think they're fascinating. They **fly pretty fast**, and they're good hunters. (**stay awake at night / see really well**)

Nadine: What do they eat?

Ming: Insects, usually. But my favorite bat is the vampire bat. They're the ones that drink blood.

Nadine: Ugh. Well, I'm writing about koalas. They're **nice and gentle**—and they don't drink blood! (**soft and furry / really cute**)

B 🎧 **4.3 Look at the chart.** Circle the correct answers below.

DESCRIBING CHARACTERISTICS AND BEHAVIOR (USING ADJECTIVES AND ADVERBS)			
Sloths are **slow** and **quiet**. Dolphins are **good** swimmers. Bees are **hard** workers.	Sloths move **slowly** and **quietly**. Dolphins swim **well**. Bees work **hard**.	*Adjectives* slow easy bad good fast hard	*Adverbs* slow**ly** eas**ily** bad**ly** **well** **fast** **hard**
How does an owl wait?	It waits **patiently**.		

1 An adjective usually comes before a verb.   T   F

2 An adverb usually comes after a verb.   T   F

3 We always make adverbs by adding -ly to adjectives.   T   F

C Complete the paragraph. Circle the correct words.

Snowy owls live in the Arctic. It's not [1] **easy / easily**
to find food there, but these [2] **beautiful / beautifully**
birds are very [3] **good / well** hunters. They wait patiently
for their prey, sitting [4] **quiet / quietly** and waiting until
they see a mouse, rabbit, or other small animal. Then
they move in [5] **quick / quickly**. Snowy owls also hear
very [6] **good / well**. This is important when they are
trying to find food under the snow.

A snowy owl in
Saskatchewan, Canada

D 🎧 4.4 Complete the conversation. Use the correct form of the words in parentheses.
Then listen and check your answers.

Anton: What are you reading?

Laura: Oh, it's a book about elephants. Did you know elephants can communicate
with other elephants up to eight kilometers away? They make a
[1] _____ (**loud**) sound with their trunks.

Anton: Wow. Do they have a [2] _____ (**good**) sense of hearing?

Laura: Yeah, but they have [3] _____ (**bad**) eyesight. I also learned that
they can't run. They just walk [4] _____ (**quick**).

Anton: I know something interesting about elephants.

Laura: What's that?

Anton: They swim really [5] _____ (**good**). I saw a video of it. It was
[6] _____ (**beautiful**).

E Work in groups. Complete the sentences about yourself. Then share your information with
the others. Suggest what animal each person is like.

1 I dance _____ .

2 I eat _____ .

3 I speak _____ .

4 I swim _____ .

5 I work _____ .

6 I sing _____ .

From your answers, I think you're like a rabbit.

I think you're more like a frog!

FUR SEAL **PUPS**

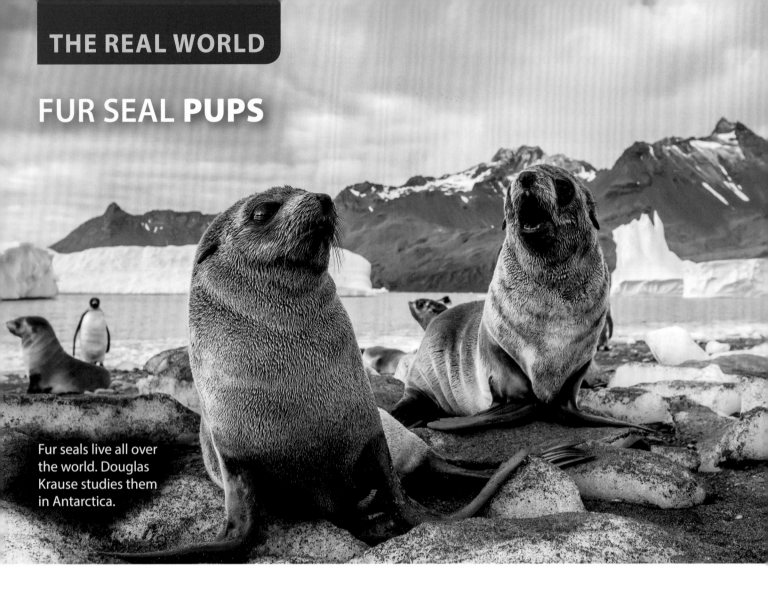

Fur seals live all over the world. Douglas Krause studies them in Antarctica.

A ▶ 4.1 **Watch the video.** Guess which words the video uses to describe fur seal pups.

curious	cute	ferocious
quiet	slow	tiny

B ▶ 4.2 **Watch the video.** Check your answers in **A**. Then circle the correct answers below.

1 Douglas Krause catches and _____ the fur seal pups.

   a feeds   **b** gives medicine to   **c** weighs

2 To catch a fur seal pup, you need to _____.

   a move slowly   **b** make eye contact   **c** speak softly

3 Douglas's favorite thing about working with fur seal pups is _____.

   a holding them   **b** watching them play   **c** watching them grow up

DO YOU KNOW?

In some languages, seals are called _____ *of the sea.*
a cats
b cows
c dogs

C Label the photo. Fur seals are different from "true" seals in a number of ways. Match the descriptions (**a–d**) with the parts of the fur seal.

a Fur seals have small outer ears.

b They use their front flippers to swim.

c They can use their rear flippers to walk.

d They have soft, thick fur.

D CRITICAL THINKING Applying **Work in groups.** The video says that fur seal pups are tiny but ferocious. Think of animals for each of these descriptions.

tiny but ferocious	small but fast	big but slow
beautiful but dangerous	scary-looking but harmless	large but gentle

PROJECT Find a picture of an animal that you like. Choose one that isn't well known. Describe the way it looks and the way it behaves.

PRONUNCIATION unstressed schwa syllables

🎧 4.5 **Listen.** Underline the unstressed schwa sound in each word. Listen again and repeat.

pat<u>ie</u>nt   around   curious   koala   gracefully   annoying

COMMUNICATION

Play charades. Work in small groups. Choose one item from each column and act out the situation. Other students guess the activity. Take turns.

A	B	C
practicing karate	quickly	in a snowstorm
making a sandwich	slowly	with a sore foot
fighting	sleepily	on a hot sidewalk
playing the drums	gracefully	underwater
singing	loudly	at a rock concert
breakdancing	softly	on a crowded bus
eating bugs	hungrily	with a heavy backpack
texting	secretly	with a runny nose

Are you playing the drums loudly underwater?

Are you fighting slowly in a snowstorm?

READING

A Discuss. Look at the title. Do you think animals can be nice? If so, give an example.

B Skim the article. Match the sentences.

1 A dog ○ ○ chased away a dangerous animal.
2 A chimpanzee ○ ○ gave food to another animal.
3 An elephant ○ ○ saved a baby animal's life.
4 A hippo ○ ○ helped a researcher.

C Scan the article. Underline the opposites of the words below.

roughly   loudly   carelessly   slowly

Rex the dog and his new friend

CAN ANIMALS BE *NICE?*

🎧 **4.6** We know that people can be nice, but what about animals?

Some scientists think they can. Animals that live in groups, like chimpanzees and elephants, have to
5 be nice to each other to **survive**. However, animals sometimes act nicely even when they don't need to. Here are four stories.

One day in southern Australia, Leonie Allan was walking her dog Rex when she **came across** a
10 dead kangaroo. A car hit it—sadly, this happened **frequently** in the area. But later that day, Rex went back to the body. There was a small baby kangaroo in its pouch! Rex pulled the baby out gently, brought it home, and placed it at Leonie's feet. He
15 saved the kangaroo's life, and the two became good friends.

Geza Teleki is a scientist who studies chimpanzees in Tanzania. One day, Geza hiked far away from his campsite. He didn't have any food with him, so he
20 tried to get some fruit from a tree. But the tree was too tall. A young chimpanzee watched Geza curiously as he tried to get to the fruit. It then climbed up the tree, picked some fruit, and gave it to Geza!

25 An elephant in Kenya hurt its trunk. It needed help because it couldn't put food into its mouth. Researcher Kayhan Ostovar watched silently. He saw the elephant show its **injured** trunk to a healthy elephant. The healthy elephant didn't
30 need any more information. It took some leaves and put them carefully into its friend's mouth.

Hippos and crocodiles live together in rivers, and they usually **get along**. But Karen Paolillo, a wildlife expert in Zimbabwe, saw something
35 interesting. One day, a crocodile tried to eat a monkey that was next to a river. A hippo ran quickly to the crocodile and **chased** it away. Why did the hippo attack the crocodile? Karen says that sometimes hippos like to protect other animals.

COMPREHENSION

A Answer the questions about *Can Animals Be Nice?*

1 MAIN IDEA What is the main idea of the article?

   a Animals that live in groups are the nicest.

   b Some animals can be nice to other animals.

   c Most animals are nice to people.

2 INFERENCE Why didn't Leonie Allan help the baby kangaroo when she saw its dead mother?

   a She didn't know it was there.

   b She thought it was already dead.

   c She thought the situation was too dangerous.

3 DETAIL We can say that Geza Teleki _____ .

   a hates hiking   **b** could not climb the tree   **c** is short

4 DETAIL Why did the elephant need help?

   a The tree was too tall.   **b** It could not use its trunk.   **c** It had no food.

5 INFERENCE What can we say about hippos?

   a They often protect monkeys.

   b They don't like crocodiles.

   c They aren't afraid of crocodiles.

B Identify causes and effects. For each statement, circle **C** (Cause) or **E** (Effect).

1 The dog saved the kangaroo's life.   **C   E**

   The dog found a kangaroo in its mother's pouch.   **C   E**

2 Teleki couldn't get fruit.   **C   E**

   The chimpanzee gave fruit to Teleki.   **C   E**

3 The elephant hurt its trunk.   **C   E**

   The healthy elephant fed the injured elephant.   **C   E**

4 The hippo attacked the crocodile.   **C   E**

   The crocodile tried to eat the monkey.   **C   E**

C CRITICAL THINKING Justifying Talk with a partner. Which animal from the article do you think was the nicest? Why?

VOCABULARY

A Find these words in the reading. Match them to their definitions.

1 **survive** ○   ○ hurt and in pain

2 **come across** ○   ○ continue living

3 **frequently** ○   ○ run after something

4 **injured** ○   ○ be friendly with each other

5 **get along** (with) ○   ○ find by chance

6 **chase** ○   ○ often

B Read the information below. Then circle the correct words to complete the sentences.

> Phrasal verbs are two- or three-word expressions that act as verbs. Here are some phrasal verbs that include the verb *come*:
>
> *come across*: find by chance   *come along*: make progress
>
> *come back*: return   *come up*: happen

1 I'm so sorry. I need to leave now, but I can come **along** / **back** later.

2 The classes are really helping. Your Spanish is coming **across** / **along** nicely.

3 I recently came **across** / **up** a beautiful old photo of my grandparents.

4 I can't go to your party because something unexpected came **up** / **back**.

WRITING

A Look at the photo. Then read the online ad.

B Prepare notes. Think of a pet that needs a new home. List words and phrases that describe its characteristics and behavior.

C Write an ad. Help the pet find a new home. Find a photo to go with your ad.

Attention Cat Lovers!

Want a cat? Why not adopt one? Chester is friendly and great with people. He loves to run around playfully and …

AMAZING **RATS**

Before You Watch

Guess. Circle **T** for True or **F** for False.

1	Rats can climb well.	T	F
2	Rats are poor swimmers.	T	F
3	Rats can hold their breath underwater for up to three minutes.	T	F

While You Watch

A ▶ 4.3 **Watch the video.** Check your answers to the exercise above.

B ▶ 4.3 **Watch again.** Label the picture. Write the names of the body parts.

claws	head	back legs	front legs	ribs	tail

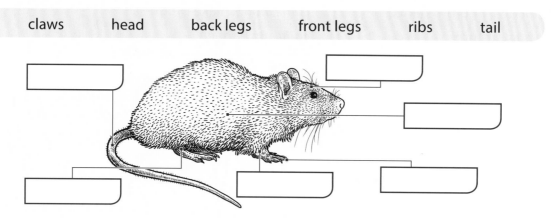

C **Complete the sentences.** Use the body parts from **B**. One is not used.

1 A rat can climb almost anything by using its _____ .

2 If a rat can get its _____ through a hole, the rest of its body will fit.

3 A rat can get through small spaces by relaxing its _____ .

4 A rat swims with its _____ .

5 When swimming, a rat uses its front legs and _____ to change direction.

After You Watch

Talk with a partner. Why do some people think that rats are a problem?

A domestic rat plays in a toy house.

REVIEW

A Read the descriptions. Which animal does each describe better?

1	slow	**sloth**	**rat**
2	playful	**crocodile**	**dolphin**
3	ferocious	**rabbit**	**lion**
4	scary	**bat**	**fur seal pup**
5	works hard	**bee**	**snake**
6	swims well	**cat**	**elephant**
7	hunts patiently	**owl**	**koala**

B Complete the sentences. Use the correct form of the words in parentheses.

1 The sloth crossed the road _____ (**slow**).

2 His pet dog is very _____ (**friendly**).

3 The monkeys were screaming _____ (**loud**).

4 Many people think rats are _____ (**ugly**), but I think they're _____ (**adorable**).

C Complete the conversation. Use the words from the box.

across	along	back	up

Peter: How's your report on bats coming [1] _____?

Camila: Not so well. I wanted to work on it over the weekend, but something came [2] _____, so I couldn't. I had to go out, and I only came [3] _____ late last night.

Peter: That's too bad. Well, I came [4] _____ this book on bats. Maybe you can use it.

Camila: Thanks! That's really nice of you.

SELF CHECK   Now I can …

☐ talk about animals and how they do things

☐ describe characteristics and behavior

☐ discuss how animals can be kind to each other

5

I'M MEETING FRIENDS LATER

A group of friends hang out after school.

PREVIEW

A 🎧 **5.1 Listen.** How do most people spend their weekends? Check (✓) the correct answers.

- ☐ reading
- ☐ doing sports
- ☐ listening to music
- ☐ watching TV
- ☐ visiting relatives
- ☐ browsing the internet

B 🎧 **5.1 Listen again.** What is each person doing this weekend?

Adam

watching _____ with his brother

having _____ with his family

playing _____ with his friends

Punitha

jogging in _____ with a friend

going to _____ for some pizza

watching _____ with her cousins

C Talk with a partner. What are you doing this weekend?

> What are you doing this weekend?

> I'm going for a swim at the beach tomorrow.

PEOPLE AND PLACES

UNIT GOALS

- talk about future events and plans
- learn how to make plans to meet people
- discover a creative way to meet people

55

LANGUAGE FOCUS

A 🎧 **5.2** **Listen and read.** What are Ming, Maya, and Nadine planning for Stig? Then repeat the conversation and replace the words in **bold**.

REAL ENGLISH   I'm afraid …

Stig: Hey, everyone! I'm glad you're all here. Are you doing anything on Saturday night?

Ming: Um, yeah. Nadine and I are **going to a basketball game. (studying for a test / working on our science project)**

Stig: Oh, OK. What about you, Maya? **Do you want to meet up**? (**What are your plans / What are you doing**)

Maya: Sorry, but **I'm afraid I'm busy.** (**I'm not free / I already have plans**)

Stig: Sure, no problem. Maybe another time. Well … see you around.

Nadine: I feel **bad. (terrible / awful)**

Ming: Me too. Should we tell him we're planning a birthday party for him?

Nadine: No. Let's keep it a surprise!

B 🎧 **5.3** **Look at the chart.** Circle the correct words to complete the sentences below.

TALKING ABOUT FUTURE EVENTS AND PLANS (USING SIMPLE PRESENT AND PRESENT PROGRESSIVE)	
Scheduled future events	**Future plans**
I **have** a class in the morning.	I**'m meeting** friends on Saturday.
The train **arrives** at 9:30.	He**'s watching** a soccer match this weekend.
What time **does** the party **start**?	What **are** you **doing** in the evening?
It **starts** at 7:00.	I**'m going** to the park.

1 We use the **simple present / present progressive** to talk about scheduled future events.

2 We use the **simple present / present progressive** to talk about future plans.

3 When answering questions about future plans, you **need / don't need** to repeat the time expression (e.g., *in the evening*).

C **Look at the signs.** Then complete the sentences using the words in the box.

GATE 12
Flight
Tokyo–Jakarta
Departure
11:45 a.m.
Arrival
5:30 p.m.

| closes | ends | arrives | leaves | opens | starts |

1 Tony's Pizza _____ at 10:00 a.m. and _____ at 11:30 p.m.

2 The flight _____ Tokyo at 11:45 a.m. and _____ in Jakarta at 5:30 p.m.

3 The movie _____ at 7:15 and _____ at 9:30.

D 🎧 5.4 **Complete the conversations.** Then listen and check your answers.

1 David: What time _____ the museum _____ (**open**)?

   Karen: At nine. I _____ (**go**) at ten. What about you?

2 Sam: What _____ you _____ (**do**) this weekend?

   Jenny: Not much. I _____ (**meet**) Erin at the mall on Saturday afternoon.
We _____ (**watch**) a movie, and then we _____ (**have**)
dinner at the Sunset Café.

3 Steve: _____ you _____ (**watch**) the soccer match? What time
does it start?

   Chris: Yes, I am. It _____ (**start**) at 7:00.

4 Fiona: _____ you _____ (**go**) anywhere this weekend?

   Celia: No. I _____ (**stay**) home. Jesse _____ (**come**) over after
her class. We might watch a movie.

E **Work in groups.** Play a memory game. Say what you are doing this weekend.

This weekend, I'm watching a movie.

This weekend, Jared is watching a movie. I'm going to the mall.

This weekend, Jared is watching a movie. Patricia is going to the mall. I'm having lunch …

THE REAL WORLD

WORLD TRAVELER

Kasha Slavner visits a school in Arusha, Tanzania.

A ▶ 5.1 **Watch the video.** At age 16, Kasha Slavner took a year off school to travel the world. Circle the correct answers to complete the sentences about her trip.

1 Kasha is traveling **on her own** / **with her mother**.

2 She's **making a documentary** / **writing a blog**.

3 She started her trip in **South America** / **South Africa**.

4 Next year, she's going to **Thailand** / **South America**.

B ▶ 5.1 **Watch again.** Check (✓) two reasons why she is traveling.

☐ to do research for a school project

☐ to meet people who are trying to bring about change

☐ to teach people photography and filmmaking skills

☐ to bring people's stories to the world

C **Work with a partner.** Kasha wants people to learn from her travels. What are some of the different ways that Kasha can tell her story? Match the words and the categories.

> talk shows   documentaries   podcasts
> social media   magazines   newspapers

online   _____   _____

print media   _____   _____

film and TV   _____   _____

D **CRITICAL THINKING Evaluating** **Talk with a partner.** Kasha took a year off school to travel the world. What are some of the benefits of doing this? Can you think of any drawbacks?

> **PROJECT Create a one-minute video.** Talk about a local issue that you think should receive more attention. Show your video to the class.

PRONUNCIATION stress in compound nouns

5.5 **Listen.** Underline the stressed word in each compound noun. What do you notice? Then listen again and repeat the words.

skateboard   airport   birthday   train station   movie theater   crowdfunding

COMMUNICATION

A **Choose three fun activities.** Use ones from the box or your own ideas.

> go bowling   go to a water park   watch a movie   meet for ice cream
> go shopping   go rock climbing   play video games   hang out at the mall

B **Find people to do the activities with you.** Complete the calendar. Write the activity and the name of the person next to the time.

> Do you want to go bowling on Saturday at two o'clock?

> I'm watching a movie with Alex at two. How about seven o'clock?

◄ ◆ ► **Saturday, November 12**

✓

10 am	
11 am	
12 pm	
1 pm	
2 pm	movie with Alex
3 pm	
4 pm	
5 pm	
6 pm	
7 pm	

A student has lunch alone in a school cafeteria.

READING

A Predict. Look at the photos and the title. What do you think the article is about?

B Skim the article. Why did Natalie create the app?
  a   for a school project
  b   to find places to eat
  c   to find people to have lunch with

C Scan the article. Who is the app for?

SIT WITH US

🎧 **5.6** You're at your new school. It's lunchtime, but you don't have anyone to sit with. You want to join someone at their table, but you're not sure if they're
5 friendly. What do you do? One student's solution was to create an app.

Natalie Hampton from California, USA, knows what it feels like to be alone at a new school. She found it difficult to
10 make new friends and had to search for a new table at lunch every day. If she sat by herself, she felt **lonely**. But if she asked to join someone and got **rejected**, she felt **embarrassed**. Her
15 solution was to create a lunch-planning app to help students like her find people to have lunch with.

Natalie Hampton and her lunch-planning app

The app—called Sit With Us—is simple. If a student is having lunch in the afternoon, they can create an invitation. Other students can open
20 the app and **accept** that invitation. They can then use the app to decide when and where to meet. This allows students to make plans online instead of face-to-face. This is the reason it works so well: it reduces the **risk** of rejection, and the embarrassment that goes along with it.

Natalie is pleased with the way people are responding to her app—
25 especially those who **suffer** from bullying. Soon after the launch of her app, she won an award for it. She also appeared in many news stories.

Natalie was even asked to speak at a United Nations Youth Assembly. In her talk, Natalie wanted people to know that you don't have to do something big to change lives. Sometimes, a simple thing—like having
30 a friend to enjoy lunch with—can make all the difference.

COMPREHENSION

A Answer the questions about *Sit With Us*.

1 **DETAIL** Which of the following statements about Natalie is true?

   a She sometimes felt lonely at school.

   b She often skipped lunch at school.

   c She made friends easily at her new school.

2 **DETAIL** What caused Natalie to feel embarrassed?

   a sitting by herself　　**b** getting rejected　　**c** using her app

3 **PURPOSE** What is the purpose of the third paragraph?

   a to explain how and why the app works

   b to show that anyone can use the app

   c to show different ways to use the app

4 **VOCABULARY** In line 25, the word *bullying* means _____.

   a being alone in a new place

   b feeling shy and embarrassed

   c treating someone in an unpleasant way

5 **PARAPHRASE** What was Natalie's message at the United Nations Youth Assembly?

   a You, and only you, can change your life.

   b Even something small can make a difference.

   c You have to think big to change people's lives.

B Check (✓) the correct answers. Which two advantages of using the app are mentioned in the article?

   ☐ The app stops bullying.

   ☐ The app helps people find friends.

   ☐ The app makes people less shy.

   ☐ The app helps people save time.

   ☐ The app helps people avoid embarrassing situations.

C CRITICAL THINKING Applying Talk with a partner.
In what other situations might an app
like *Sit With Us* be useful?

VOCABULARY

A Find these words in the article. Then circle the correct answer.

1 A **lonely** person probably *has / doesn't have* a lot of friends.

2 If you **reject** something, you *want / do not want* it.

3 You would probably feel **embarrassed** after *passing an exam / forgetting someone's name*.

4 If you **accept** an invitation, you say *yes / no* to it.

5 A **risk** refers to the chance of a *good / bad* thing happening.

6 When you **suffer** from something, it affects you in a *nice / bad* way.

B Read the information below. Then complete the sentences by adding *-ed* or *-ing*.

> Adjectives ending with *-ed* and *-ing* can be confusing.
>
> Adjectives ending in *-ed* describe how people feel: *I am embarrassed*.
>
> Adjectives ending in *-ing* describe what causes the feeling: *My results are embarrassing*.

1 He was surpris_____ that so many people showed up for lunch.

2 I was worried that the movie would be bor_____, but it wasn't.

3 I'm so annoy_____. Josh is always late, and he never says sorry.

4 This app isn't confus_____. It's really easy to use.

IDIOM

If you are _____, you are unable to speak because you are shy or embarrassed.
a mouth-mashed
b brain-blanked
c tongue-tied

WRITING

A Read the email.

B Prepare a timetable for Saturday. List what you are doing and when. Leave a few hours empty.

C Write an email to a friend. Make plans to meet. Say what you are doing and when you are free.

New message

To Lina@mail.com

Subject Plans for Saturday

Hi Lina,   July 14

What time would you like to meet on Saturday? I'm pretty busy that day, but I have some spare time. In the morning, I'm going to the mall with Jacob. Then, I'm going bowling with …

Send

THE *BOILING* RIVER

Before You Watch

Look at the photo. Why do you think the water is hot?
Have you heard of rivers or lakes that are hot like this?

While You Watch

A ▶ 5.2 **Watch Part 1 of the video.** Circle the correct answers.

1 The Boiling River is in **Brazil** / **Peru**.

2 Andrés **heard stories about** / **swam in** the Boiling River when he was young.

3 Andrés first heard that the Boiling River was real from **his aunt** / **a scientist**.

4 You can swim in the Boiling River **in the evening** / **after a storm**.

B ▶ 5.3 **Watch Part 2 of the video.** Circle **T** for True or **F** for False.

1 Andrés is going to the Boiling River alone.   T   F

2 Andrés studies the Earth's volcanic heat.   T   F

3 Andrés wants to use the river's heat to create electricity.   T   F

4 The water from the river is poisonous.   T   F

5 The locals support Andrés's research.   T   F

C **Why is the Boiling River important?** Check (✓) three reasons Andrés gives.

☐ Its water has special chemicals in it.   ☐ It isn't found in a volcanic area.

☐ It's the only hot river in the world.   ☐ It's culturally important.

☐ The wildlife there is special.   ☐ It's great for tourism.

After You Watch

Look at the reasons in C. Do you think tourists should be
allowed to visit the Boiling River? Why or why not?

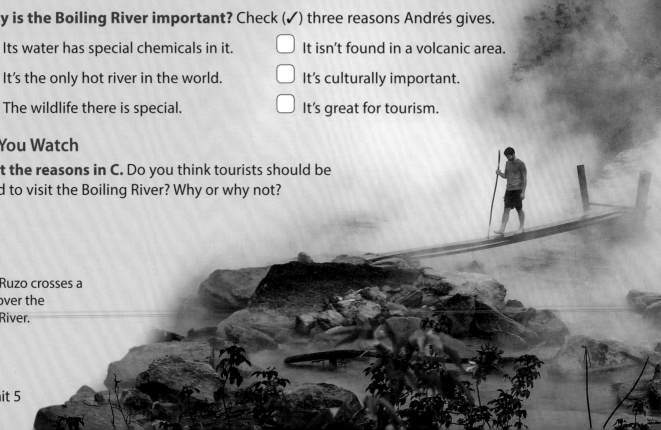

Andrés Ruzo crosses a
bridge over the
Boiling River.

A Match the words.

1 plan   ◯   ◯ a movie
2 browse   ◯   ◯ a party
3 study for   ◯   ◯ the internet
4 watch   ◯   ◯ a test

5 accept   ◯   ◯ bowling
6 play   ◯   ◯ a project
7 work on   ◯   ◯ an invitation
8 go   ◯   ◯ video games

B Complete the sentences. Use the correct form of the verbs.

1 _____ you _____ (**do**) anything fun this weekend?

2 What time _____ your flight _____ (**arrive**) tonight?

3 We _____ (**have**) dinner with Claudia and Rex next week.

4 The concert _____ (**start**) at 7 p.m. It _____ (**end**) at 10 p.m.

5 I _____ (**not meet**) Talia tomorrow. I _____ (**go**) for a run.

C Complete the sentences. Circle the correct answers.

1 I was so **surprised** / **surprising** when Jan came to the party a day early.

2 Sid can be **annoyed** / **annoying** when he talks too loudly!

3 I called him by the wrong name. It was so **embarrassed** / **embarrassing**!

4 This play is very **confused** / **confusing**. I have no idea what's happening.

5 Everyone says this movie is great, but I got **bored** / **boring** halfway through.

SELF CHECK   Now I can …

☐ talk about future events and plans

☐ make plans to meet people

☐ discuss a creative way to meet people

WHAT WILL EARTH BE LIKE IN THE FUTURE?

Lake Wallace, Australia, after a long period of dry weather in 2016

PREVIEW

A Use a dictionary. Write ↑ for words that mean "become larger." Write ↓ for words that mean "become smaller."

_____ increase   _____ fall

_____ rise   _____ shrink

_____ decrease   _____ expand

B 🎧 **6.1 Guess.** How will climate change affect Earth? Circle the correct answers. Then listen and check.

1 Temperatures will **fall / rise**.

2 Freshwater levels will **fall / rise**.

3 Wildfires will **increase / decrease**.

4 Deserts will **shrink / expand**.

5 Farmland will **shrink / expand**.

6 Food supplies will **increase / decrease**.

C Talk with a partner. What are some other possible effects of climate change?

> I think ocean levels will rise in the future.

> Yeah. And I think cities will …

THE NATURAL WORLD

UNIT GOALS

- find out how climate change will affect us

- learn language for making predictions

- explore ways to fight climate change

LANGUAGE FOCUS

A 🎧6.2 **Listen and read.** What will happen when farmlands shrink? Then repeat the conversation and replace the words in **bold**.

REAL ENGLISH	Are you serious?

Stig: Do you think temperatures will **rise** a lot in the future? (**go up / increase**)

Nadine: Yes, I do. Climate change is a very serious problem.

Stig: Hmm. How will it affect us?

Nadine: Well, when it gets hotter, **farmlands will shrink.** (**freshwater levels will fall / deserts will expand**)

Stig: And what will happen when **farmlands shrink**? (**freshwater levels fall / deserts expand**)

Nadine: Do you really want to know?

Stig: Sure!

Nadine: **There'll be less food.** (**Food supplies will decrease / There won't be enough food**)

Stig: What? Are you serious? We have to stop climate change now!

B 🎧6.3 **Look at the chart.** Circle the correct words to complete the sentences below.

MAKING PREDICTIONS (USING *WILL*, *WON'T*, *MORE*, *FEWER*, AND *LESS*)	
What **will** the future **be like**?	It**'ll be** hotter and drier. There**'ll be more** wildfires. There**'ll be more** pollution. There**'ll be fewer** animals. There**'ll be less** food.
Will there **be** a lot more people?	Yes, there **will**. There**'ll** (definitely) **be** a lot more people. No, there **won't**. There (probably) **won't be** a lot more people.
Do you think food prices **will increase**?	Yes, I do. I think they**'ll increase**. No, I don't. I don't think they**'ll increase**.

1 We use *fewer* before **countable / uncountable / countable and uncountable** nouns.

2 We use *less* before **countable / uncountable / countable and uncountable** nouns.

3 We use *more* before **countable / uncountable / countable and uncountable** nouns.

C 🎧 **6.4 Complete the passage.** Use *will* and the words from the box. Then listen and check.

be	disappear	hold	go	(not) be	melt	need	rise

Climate change is a very real problem for the people of the Maldives. Scientists think it's likely that—sometime this century—the island nation [1] _____ because of climate change. Ice [2] _____, and ocean levels [3] _____. This [4] _____ a huge problem for the country. On average, its islands are only 1.3 meters above sea level. Because ocean levels rise a little bit every year, many people [5] _____ able to stay in their homes. No one knows where they [6] _____, but they [7] _____ to find a new place to live. To draw attention to their problem, the government held a meeting underwater. They joked that it's where they [8] _____ their meetings in the future.

D **Complete the predictions.** Use *more*, *fewer*, or *less*. Then discuss the predictions. Which do you think will happen? Which won't?

1 There will be more deserts and _____ drinking water in the future.

2 Gas-burning cars are becoming less popular. There will be _____ electric cars.

3 Deforestation will remain a problem. There will be _____ trees in our forests.

4 Land for agriculture will shrink. There will be _____ food for people to eat.

5 Space travel will become cheaper, so _____ people will travel to space.

6 There will be _____ environmental problems. Technology will help fix them.

E **Turn to page 150.** Are you an optimist or a pessimist? Take a survey to find out.

Maldives government officials prepare for an underwater meeting.

SIX DEGREES

Mark Lynas is a climate change expert
and the author of the book *Six Degrees*.

A ▶ 6.1 **Predict.** What do you think will happen when Earth's
temperature increases by 1°C, 2°C, and 3°C? Work with a partner.
Then watch the video and check your answers.

1 1°C ○   ○ The Amazon rainforest might burn down.

2 2°C ○   ○ Sea levels will rise.

3 3°C ○   ○ Most of our coral reefs will disappear.

B ▶ 6.1 **Watch again.** Check (✓) three things Mark says we can do to
reduce or adapt to global warming.

☐ eat less meat and dairy products   ☐ grow more genetically modified crops

☐ use less oil and natural gas   ☐ use more wind and solar energy

☐ avoid nuclear power   ☐ build more electric vehicles

DO YOU KNOW?

Which of these
contributes the
most to climate
change?
a farming
b factories
c transportation

C **Work with a partner.** The temperature increase Mark describes is caused by greenhouse gases. Complete the paragraph about greenhouse gases using the words in the box.

activity   fuel   reduce   produce   keep

Greenhouse gases trap heat in the air and ¹ _____ the Earth warm. Sadly, human
² _____ is increasing the amount of greenhouse gas in our atmosphere. Carbon dioxide
is the main greenhouse gas. We release it when we cut down trees and burn ³ _____ .
Methane is another common greenhouse gas. This comes mainly from cow farming and
transporting oil and gas. Humans ⁴ _____ many other greenhouse gases. To fight global
warming, we have to ⁵ _____ the amount of greenhouse gas we release.

D CRITICAL THINKING Evaluating **Talk with a partner.** Do you think Mark's suggestions for dealing with global warming are good ones? Can you think of any downsides?

PROJECT Find out more about carbon footprints. List three ways to reduce your carbon footprint. Then rank them from *easiest to do* (1) to *hardest to do* (3).

PRONUNCIATION reduction of *will*

🎧 6.5 **Listen.** Write the words you hear. Listen again and repeat the sentences.

1 _____ buy fewer things and recycle more.

2 _____ only drive electric cars in the future.

3 _____ help fight global warming.

4 _____ find a way to reduce pollution.

COMMUNICATION

Work in groups. Choose a topic and a time. Predict what will happen. Find out if your group members agree or disagree.

Topic	Time
the environment	in the next year or two
technology	in five years
transportation	in the next 10 to 20 years
education	by 2040
medicine	within 50 years
entertainment	in my lifetime
energy	sometime this century
pollution	in 500 years

In five years, I think people will fly to work.

I think five years is too soon. But it will probably happen in my lifetime.

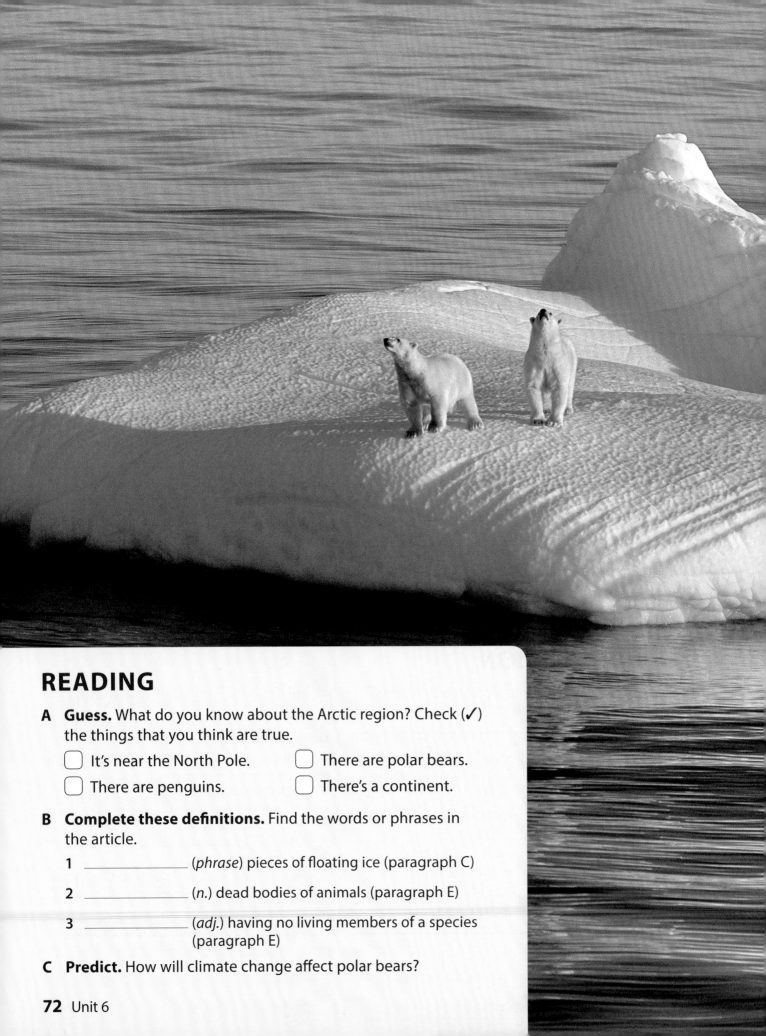

READING

A Guess. What do you know about the Arctic region? Check (✓) the things that you think are true.

- ☐ It's near the North Pole.
- ☐ There are penguins.
- ☐ There are polar bears.
- ☐ There's a continent.

B Complete these definitions. Find the words or phrases in the article.

1 _____ (*phrase*) pieces of floating ice (paragraph C)

2 _____ (*n.*) dead bodies of animals (paragraph E)

3 _____ (*adj.*) having no living members of a species (paragraph E)

C Predict. How will climate change affect polar bears?

Photographer Paul Nicklen took this photograph of two polar bears on an ice floe.

ON THIN ICE

A 🎧 **6.6** Paul Nicklen waited patiently on a sheet of Arctic ice. He was there to take pictures for *National Geographic*. Suddenly, he saw something move. It was a polar bear, swimming in the icy water toward a seal.

B Paul lay down on the ice to get a better photo. The bear jumped out of the water to catch the seal. Unfortunately, the ice **cracked**, and the bear fell back into the water. The polar bear couldn't get its meal and had to swim farther away to find food.

C The polar bear's story is unfortunately becoming more **familiar**. To understand why, you need to know a few things about the Arctic. First, it is mostly ocean. Second, a lot of this ocean is covered by ice. This ice is **vital** to the survival of many Arctic animals. Polar bears, for example, use the ice to hunt seals, their favorite meal. They stand on the ice floes and wait for them to come up for air.

D However, because of climate change, Arctic temperatures are rising and the ice is becoming thinner. This makes finding food more difficult for the bears. As the Arctic ice melts, polar bears have to swim farther to find thicker ice—sometimes more than 200 kilometers. Some polar bears cannot swim that far and, sadly, they **drown**.

E On his last trip, Paul saw three polar bear carcasses. Before climate change became a serious problem, a dead bear was a rare sight. Wildlife experts think that climate change will have a terrible effect on polar bears. In the future, polar ice will continue to shrink, and this will **endanger** them. Some scientists believe that 65 percent of the world's polar bears will disappear by 2050. In other words, these beautiful **creatures** are in danger of becoming extinct.

COMPREHENSION

A Answer the questions about *On Thin Ice*.

1 **MAIN IDEA** What is the main idea of the article?

   a There are fewer seals for polar bears to hunt.

   b Arctic temperatures are rising.

   c Climate change is endangering polar bears.

2 **DETAIL** The polar bear Paul Nicklen saw couldn't catch the seal because _____.

   a it made too much noise   **b** the ice was too thin   **c** the seal was too quick

3 **DETAIL** How do polar bears usually hunt seals?

   a They wait on ice floes.   **b** They wait in the water.   **c** They drown the seals.

4 **VOCABULARY** In paragraph E, *a rare sight* refers to something that _____.

   a is horrible to look at   **b** you don't see often   **c** is blind

5 **INFERENCE** According to the article, which of these statements is true?

   a Climate change will still be a problem in 2050.

   b Polar ice will disappear completely by 2050.

   c Polar bears have to hunt different animals to survive.

IDIOM

If you are "on thin ice," you are _____.

a strong and powerful
b in a risky situation
c always changing

B Complete the flow chart. Write the effects of climate change in the correct order.

  a Some polar bears drown.

  b Polar ice melts.

  c Temperatures rise.

  d Polar bears become endangered.

  e Polar bears have to swim farther between ice floes.

  f Ice breaks into ice floes.

1 _____ → 2 _____ → 3 _____ → 4 _____ → 5 _____ → 6 _____

C **CRITICAL THINKING Inferring** **Talk with a partner.**
What other animals are affected by climate change? Can you think of ways to help them?

Greta Thunberg became an environmental activist after learning about polar bears and climate change in school.

VOCABULARY

A **Find these words in the article.** Then complete the sentences.

> crack   familiar   vital   drown   endanger   creature

1 If you don't wear your life jacket, you could _____ .

2 Don't drive too fast or you'll _____ the lives of other motorists.

3 The walrus is a large marine _____ with two large teeth.

4 The ice is thin. It will _____ if you stand on it.

5 I don't know his name, but he looks _____ .

6 It is _____ we work together to fight climate change.

B **Read the information below.** Then complete the sentences. Use the words in the box with the suffix -y. Check your spelling in a dictionary.

> The suffix -y can be added to some nouns to make them adjectives.
> For example:
>
> water → watery
>
> ice → icy

> luck   mud   noise   rain

1 On _____ days, I like to stay home and read.

2 I find it hard to concentrate when it's _____ .

3 Please leave your boots outside if they're _____ .

4 She was _____ that the hotel still had one room left.

WRITING

A **Read the paragraph.**

B **What will your town or city be like in 25 years?** Make notes.

C **Write a paragraph.** Say what your city is like now, and what you think it will be like in 25 years.

My city will be very different in 25 years. It's a popular place to live now, but I think more people will move …

RENEWABLE ENERGY

Before You Watch

What are some popular types of renewable energy? Match the words with the pictures.

solar   wind   biomass   hydro   geothermal

1 _____ 2 _____ 3 _____ 4 _____ 5 _____

While You Watch

A ▶ 6.2 **Watch Part 1 of the video.** How much of our energy comes from renewable sources?

   a 10%   **b** 40%   **c** 60%

B ▶ 6.3 **Watch Part 2 of the video.** Then complete the sentences. Use the words in the box.

climate change   disrupts   generates   intermittent   pollution   reliable

Positives	Downsides
1 Renewable energy will help us combat _____ .	4 It _____ power on a smaller scale than fossil fuels.
2 It will help decrease _____ .	5 It sometimes _____ wildlife and migration patterns.
3 It is a(n) _____ power source. It never runs out.	6 Some sources are _____ . Some days, you get less sun and wind.

C **Look at the chart.** Then circle the correct answers.

  1 **Hydro / Solar** energy is the most popular renewable energy source.

  2 **Geothermal / Wood** is the least popular renewable energy source.

  3 **Waste / Wind** generates about as much energy as biomass.

SOLAR GEOTHERMAL WASTE HYDRO-ELECTRIC WIND WOOD BIOMASS

After You Watch

Talk with a partner. Which type of renewable energy has the most potential? Why?

A wind farm generates electricity next to a tulip field in Flevoland, Holland.

A Complete the predictions. Circle the correct answers.

1 Greenhouse gases will **produce** / **trap** more heat.

2 Global temperatures will **expand** / **rise** in the next few years.

3 Farmland will **fall** / **shrink** and we'll have less food.

4 Polar ice will **drown** / **melt** sometime this century.

5 Human activity will **endanger** / **reduce** more creatures.

6 We'll use more **renewable** / **nuclear** energy, like solar and wind.

B Unscramble the words to make predictions.

1 wildfires / there / will / more / be

_____

2 will / fewer / animals / there / be

_____

3 be / different / the / won't / future / very

_____

4 less / there / be / definitely / food / will

_____

5 probably / cars / won't / fossil fuels / use

_____

C Complete the sentences. Add the suffix -*y* to the nouns.

> luck   mud   noise   rain

1 He came home with _____ shoes.

2 He couldn't hear me because the train was _____ .

3 I like to stay in on _____ days.

4 He was _____ to catch the last bus.

SELF CHECK   Now I can …

☐ describe how climate change will affect us

☐ use language for making predictions

☐ talk about ways to fight climate change

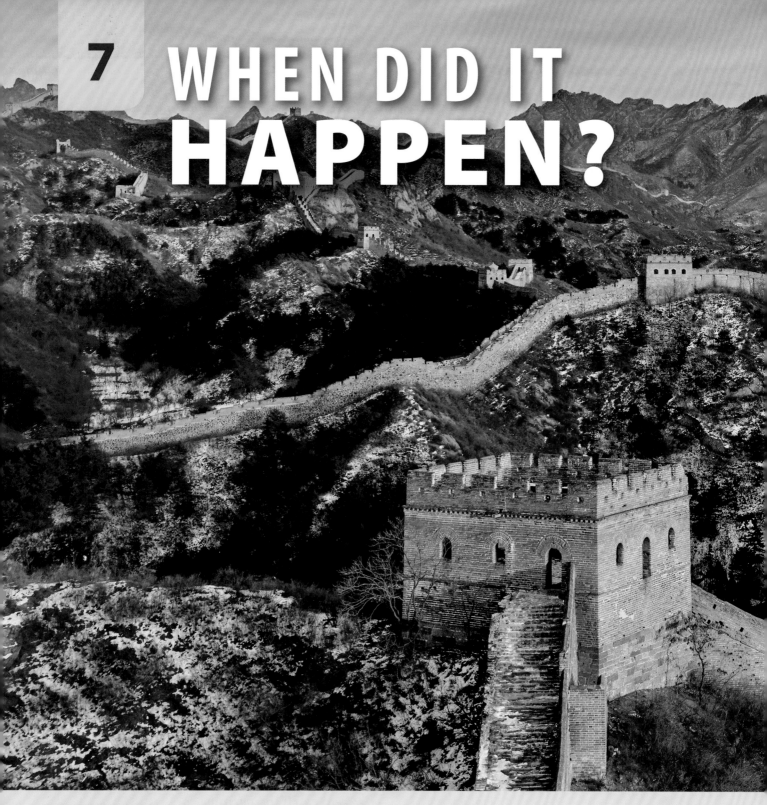

7 WHEN DID IT HAPPEN?

PREVIEW

A 🎧 **7.1** **Listen to a quiz.** Guess when the events happened.

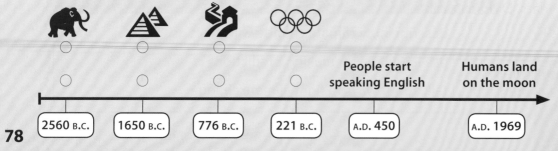

				People start speaking English	Humans land on the moon
2560 B.C.	1650 B.C.	776 B.C.	221 B.C.	A.D. 450	A.D. 1969

A section of The Great Wall,
Hebei Province, China

HISTORY AND CULTURE

UNIT GOALS

- explore key events in human history

- learn to talk about past and historical events

- find out about historical figures and their achievements

B 🎧 7.2 **Listen to part 2 of the quiz.** Match the pictures to the years. Did any of the answers surprise you?

C **Work with a partner.** Think of five important historical events. Find out when they happened. Then quiz another pair.

LANGUAGE FOCUS

A 🎧 **7.3** **Listen and read.** When was Ming in New York? Then repeat the conversation and replace the words in **bold**.

> **REAL ENGLISH** What a disaster!

Nadine: Hey, Ming. Is that you in this picture?

Ming: Yeah, that's me in preschool. My hair was **a mess!** (**so messy / such a mess**)

Nadine: Really? You think so?

Ming: Can't you tell? Here's another photo of me in middle school. Look at my hair. **What a disaster!** (**It's awful / It looks terrible**)

Nadine: Um, I think it looks fine. What about this photo? When **did you go to** New York? (**did you visit / were you in**)

Ming: A year ago. I was there for two weeks. My hair's terrible in that photo, too.

Nadine: You know … your hairstyle **never changes.** (**isn't any different now / always looks the same**)

Ming: What? That's not true!

B 🎧 **7.4** **Look at the chart.** Circle the correct words to complete the sentences below.

TALKING ABOUT PAST EVENTS (USING *WHEN, HOW LONG,* AND PREPOSITIONS OF TIME)	
A point in time	
When was the first soccer World Cup final?	It was **in** 1930. / It was **on** July 30, 1930.
How long ago were the first Olympic Games?	They were over 2,700 years **ago**.
A period of time	
When did Cleopatra live?	She lived **from** 69 B.C. **to** 30 B.C.
How long was Marco Polo in China?	He was there **for** 17 years.

1 We use *on* to specify a **year / date**.

2 We use *ago* to specify a **point in time / period of time** in the past.

3 We use *for* to state **when something happened / how long something lasted**.

C 🎧 7.5 **Complete the conversation.** Use the words in the box. You can use them more than once. Then listen and check.

| ago | for | from | in | on | to |

Zoe: You're a fan of the Star Wars movies, aren't you?

Eric: I'm a *huge* fan. Why?

Zoe: When did the first one come out?

Eric: It was released [1] _____ 1977. I can actually tell you the exact date. It came out [2] _____ May 25, 1977.

Zoe: How did you know that? That's over 40 years [3] _____ !

Eric: I told you—I'm a huge fan. The movie was so big. After its release, it quickly became the most successful movie ever. Movie theaters continued to show it [4] _____ many years.

Zoe: Wow. When did the next two movies come out?

Eric: *The Empire Strikes Back* came out [5] _____ 1980, and *Return of the Jedi* came out [6] _____ 1983. But there were no movies [7] _____ 1984 [8] _____ 1998.

Zoe: Yeah, I remember watching *The Phantom Menace* many years [9] _____ . They made a few other movies recently, too. I really enjoyed *Rogue One*!

D **Work with a partner.** Unscramble the words to make questions. Can you guess the answers?

1 when / sink / did / the *Titanic* _____?

2 the first / was / when / Harry Potter movie _____?

3 when / iPhone / Apple / did / the first / make _____?

4 president / was / Barack Obama / how long _____?

5 the moon landing / how long / was / ago _____?

E **Work in groups.** Write five memorable things that happened in your life. Use these ideas, or your own. Then share your lists and ask each other questions.

started school	took part in a contest	won an award
met your best friend	got your first cell phone	played in a band
did a part-time job	traveled to an interesting place	lived in a different country

I got my first cell phone three years ago.

What kind of phone did you get?

THE **SPACE** RACE

American astronaut Buzz Aldrin
walks on the moon.

A ▶ 7.1 **Watch the video.** Complete the dates.

1 195_____ — The Soviet Union sent its first satellite into space.

2 196_____ — Yuri Gagarin became the first person to travel to space.

3 196_____ — Alan Shepard became the first American to travel to space.

4 196_____ — John Glenn flew around the Earth three times.

5 196_____ — Two men walked on the moon.

B ▶ 7.1 **Watch again.** Circle the correct answers.

1 The first human-made satellite was called **Apollo** / **Sputnik**.

2 The first person in space was from **the Soviet Union** / **the United States**.

3 The first American to orbit Earth was **Alan Shepard** / **John Glenn**.

4 The first person to walk on the moon was **Neil Armstrong** / **Buzz Aldrin**.

C Complete the paragraph. Use the words in the box.

> companies   countries   moon   satellites   tourism

The original space race is over, but today, there's a new space race. New players are competing to visit the ¹ _____ , Mars, and even distant asteroids. China, Japan, and other ² _____ are expanding their space programs. Some ³ _____ like Boeing and SpaceX are launching ⁴ _____ into space. And others, like Virgin and Blue Origin, are trying to make space ⁵ _____ popular so that regular people can experience space.

D CRITICAL THINKING Interpreting Talk with a partner. Read Yuri Gagarin's quote below. What do you think he means?

> "Looking at the Earth from afar, you realize it is too small for conflict and just big enough for cooperation."

PROJECT Research space tourism. Find out how much it costs to go to space as a tourist. Would you spend money to travel to space? Why or why not?

PRONUNCIATION syllable stress

🎧 7.6 **Listen.** Underline the stressed syllable. Then listen again and repeat the words.

1 <u>his</u>tory	historical	4 technology	technological
2 explore	exploration	5 compete	competition
3 celebrate	celebration	6 educate	education

COMMUNICATION

Play a trivia game. Work in groups of three. **Student A:** Go to page 151. **Student B:** Go to page 153. **Student C:** Go to page 154.

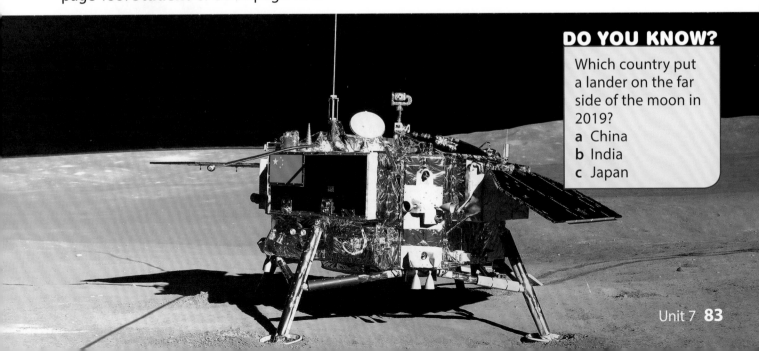

DO YOU KNOW?
Which country put a lander on the far side of the moon in 2019?
a China
b India
c Japan

READING

A Skim the article. Choose a different title.

  a A Body in the Sea

  b Mystery on the Mountain

  c The Ice Age Family

B Match the words with the pictures.

arrows   ax   knife

1 _____   2 _____   3 _____

C Scan the article. Which item in **B** killed Ötzi?

An actor plays Ötzi in
the 2017 movie, *Iceman*.

AN *ANCIENT* MURDER

🎧 7.7   In 1991, hikers in the Italian Alps discovered a body frozen in ice. They were surprised to learn that it **belonged** to a man who died 5,300 years ago! This was the oldest complete human body ever found.

Scientists named the man Ötzi, after the place he was found. They
5   studied his body and learned many things. His teeth and skull showed that he was probably in his 40s. He wore thick clothes and shoes made of bearskin. He carried a stone knife, wooden arrows, and equipment for starting fires. And he had a copper ax—a rare and **valuable** tool back when Ötzi was alive.

10   **The Plot Thickens**

Most interestingly, there were injuries on Ötzi's body that showed he was attacked. There was a piece from a stone arrow **buried** deep in his left shoulder. Scientists believe this is what killed him. There was also the blood of four other people on his clothes, as well as injuries on his
15   hands. These injuries were not completely healed—they were recent, but not as recent as the injury on his shoulder.

Ötzi's story quickly became a murder mystery—the world's oldest murder mystery. Why was he killed? Was he running away when he died? And why was he even there, in such a cold and remote place?
20   New studies in 2010 and 2018 revealed more **clues**.

New Findings

Scientists learned that Ötzi ate a big meal right before he died—they found goat and deer meat in his stomach. He was therefore probably resting, not running, when he died. They also learned that the arrow in
25   Ötzi's shoulder hit him from behind.

Did someone injure Ötzi in a fight, and did Ötzi run up the mountain to **escape**? Did that same person follow Ötzi up the mountain and shoot him in the back? It's a good **theory**, but scientists will probably never completely know how or why Ötzi died.

COMPREHENSION

A Answer the questions about *An Ancient Murder*.

IDIOM

If you "get away with murder,"
you _____ for your actions.
a take responsibility
b avoid punishment
c become famous

1 **INFERENCE** The copper ax tell us that Ötzi was
probably _____ .

   a a great hunter

   b someone important

   c a metal worker

2 **VOCABULARY** What does the expression *the plot thickens* mean?

   a The situation becomes more serious.

   b The situation becomes more mysterious.

   c The mystery is solved.

3 **REFERENCE** What does *this* in line 13 refer to?

   a his left shoulder   b a violent death   c a piece of stone

4 **DETAIL** What did scientists find that changed their thoughts about Ötzi?

   a food in his stomach   b injuries on his hand   c blood on his clothes

5 **DETAIL** What DON'T scientists know about Ötzi?

   a his age   b what he ate   c who killed him

B Add the events to the timeline. Write the letters (**a–f**).

a Ötzi froze in the ice.

b Ötzi died.

c Ötzi ate a large meal.

d Ötzi hurt his hands in a fight.

e Ötzi ran into the mountains.

f Someone attacked Ötzi with an arrow.

1 _____   2 _____   3 _____   4 _____   5 _____   6 _____

C **CRITICAL THINKING Evaluating** Talk with a partner. Read the sentences about Ötzi. Some are true statements. Others are speculation. Write **F** for Fact or **S** for Speculation.

1 _____ He was someone important.

2 _____ He wore clothes made of bearskin.

3 _____ He had a knife, arrows, and an ax.

4 _____ He ate goat and deer meat.

5 _____ He was resting when he died.

6 _____ He was shot from behind.

VOCABULARY

A **Find the words below in the article.** Then match the two parts of the sentences.

1 If an item **belongs** to you, ○ ○ it shows more about what happened.

2 If something is **valuable**, ○ ○ you are able to get away from it.

3 If an object is **buried**, ○ ○ it is yours.

4 If an object is a **clue**, ○ ○ it tries to explain something.

5 If you **escape** from something, ○ ○ it is expensive.

6 An idea is a **theory** if ○ ○ it is deep inside something.

B **Read the information below.** Then circle the general noun and add a specific noun to each group.

> **General nouns** are groups or categories. For example:
> *Tools* are equipment that help you do tasks more easily.
> **Specific nouns** are objects within those categories. For example:
> *Arrows*, *axes*, and *knives* are types of tools.

Example: ax / hammer / (tool)   _____saw_____

1 copper / material / stone   _____

2 chopsticks / spoon / utensil   _____

3 knife / sword / weapon   _____

4 gadget / laptop / cell phone   _____

WRITING

A **Read the biography.**

B **Think of someone you admire.** List important dates, events, and achievements in that person's life.

C **Write a short biography.**

Naomi Osaka is a very successful tennis player. She was born in Japan in 1997, but she moved to the United States when she was …

THE *UNSINKABLE* SHIP

Before You Watch

Take a quiz. What do you know about the *Titanic*? Circle your answers.

1 The *Titanic* sank in **1912** / **1948**.

2 The *Titanic* sailed from **England** / **the United States**.

3 The *Titanic* crashed into **another ship** / **an iceberg**.

While You Watch

A ▶ 7.2 **Watch Part 1 of the video.** Circle the correct answers.

1 The *Titanic* had **good** / **poor** safety features for the time.

2 The crew **did many** / **didn't do any** safety drills.

3 There were **20** / **48** lifeboats on the *Titanic*.

4 The owner didn't want the *Titanic* to look **luxurious** / **messy**.

B ▶ 7.3 **Watch Part 2 of the video.** Then number the events in order (1–5).

_____ The ship received six warning messages.

_____ Many passengers died because there weren't enough lifeboats.

_____ The crew saw the iceberg, but it was too late.

_____ The ship entered dangerous icy waters.

_____ The captain turned the ship but didn't slow down.

C **What mistakes led to the disaster?** Check (✓) the correct answers.

☐ The owner built the ship using cheap materials.

☐ People thought that the *Titanic* could not sink.

☐ The captain sailed too quickly in icy waters.

After You Watch

Talk with a partner. Do you think accidents like this can happen again? What can we do to prevent them?

A Complete the sentences. Use the words from the box.

| ax | clue | history | mystery | theory | satellite |

1 Scientists aren't sure if his _____ is correct.

2 Sputnik was the first human-made _____.

3 He used his _____ to cut down the tree.

4 Nobody knows how the ancient Egyptians built the pyramids. It's a(n) _____.

5 He doesn't know what happened, but he found an important _____.

6 We need to learn from _____ so that we don't repeat our mistakes.

B Circle the correct words.

1 When **were / did** the Seoul Olympics take place?

2 Robert Ballard found the remains of the *Titanic* **in / on** 1985.

3 The first successful airplane flight was **in / on** December 17, 1903.

4 The last mammoth died about 3,700 years **before / ago**.

5 Cleopatra ruled Egypt **for / from** almost 30 years.

6 **When / How long** did Napoleon die?

C Match the general nouns to the specific nouns.

1 gadgets ○   ○ hammer, screwdriver, saw

2 materials ○   ○ knives, guns, swords

3 tools ○   ○ spoons, forks, chopsticks

4 utensils ○   ○ cell phones, tablets, laptops

5 weapons ○   ○ stone, wood, plastic

The *Titanic* just before its first and final voyage

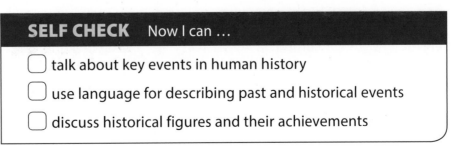

SELF CHECK   Now I can …

☐ talk about key events in human history

☐ use language for describing past and historical events

☐ discuss historical figures and their achievements

HAVE YOU EVER TRIED GO-KARTING?

PREVIEW

A 🎧 8.1 **Listen to three friends talk.** Match the people to the experiences.

1	Katy	○	○ surfing	○	○	last weekend
2	Brian	○	○ bungee jumping	○	○	last summer
3	Michiko	○	○ go-karting	○	○	two years ago

B 🎧 8.1 **Listen again.** When did each person do each thing? Match the time periods.

An indoor go-kart track in Valencia, Spain

C **Talk with a partner.** Which activity in **A** would you most like to try? What other sports would you like to try?

> I'd most like to try go-karting.

> Me too. And maybe surfing as well.

UNIT GOALS

• learn about interesting people and what they've done

• use language for talking about life experiences

• think about things you want achieve in your lifetime

LANGUAGE FOCUS

A 🎧 **8.2 Listen and read.** Why is Nadine asking Maya so many questions? Then repeat the conversation and replace the words in **bold**.

REAL ENGLISH What's going on?

Nadine:	Have you been to the **aquarium** here in town? (**zoo / amusement park**)
Maya:	Yes, I have. I've been there twice.
Nadine:	Oh. Have you ever had Moroccan food?
Maya:	Sure. Don't you remember? We **tried it at the street fair** last year. (**had it at a café / got some from a food truck**)
Nadine:	Hmm. Have you ever tried **indoor rock climbing**? (**parasailing / bungee jumping**)
Maya:	No, I haven't. And I don't **think I'd enjoy it**. What's going on, Nadine? Why are you asking me all these questions? (**have any plans to / ever want to**)
Nadine:	Um … Your birthday is next week, and I don't know where to take you!

B 🎧 **8.3 Look at the chart.** Read the sentences below and circle **T** for True or **F** for False.

TALKING ABOUT PAST EXPERIENCES (USING PRESENT PERFECT)	
Have you **ever had** Moroccan food?	Yes, I **have**. I**'ve had** it several times. No, I **haven't**. I**'ve never** tried it.
Has she **tried** indoor rock climbing?	Yes, she **has**. She went last year. No, she **hasn't**. She**'s** never **done** it.
I**'ve been** to the zoo a couple of times.	Me too. / I **have**, too. Oh, really? I **haven't**.
He**'s never gone** surfing.	Me neither. / Neither **have** I. Oh, really? I **have**.

1 We can use the present perfect to describe things we have never done. **T**   **F**

2 We can use the present perfect to say how many times we did something. **T**   **F**

3 We use the present perfect to say when we did something. **T**   **F**

C **Match the phrases.** Then ask and answer questions with a partner. **Have you ever … ?**

played	○ ○	Spanish food	seen	○ ○	carrot juice	ridden	○ ○	fishing
eaten	○ ○	table tennis	done	○ ○	a 3-D movie	gone	○ ○	a password
gotten	○ ○	an A+	drunk	○ ○	volunteer work	forgotten	○ ○	a horse

Have you ever played table tennis?

No, I haven't. Have you?

D 🎧 **8.4** **Complete the conversations.** Use the correct form of the verbs. Then listen and check your answers.

1 **Pablo:** ¹ _____ you _____ (**ever try**) zip-lining?

 Julie: No, I haven't. But my older sister ² _____ (**do**) it several times.

 Pablo: A friend invited me to try it next week. I don't know if I'll like it.

 Julie: You'll never know if you don't try!

2 **Kurt:** I ³ _____ (**never have**) Turkish food before. Have you?

 Jing: Yeah, I have. it's delicious. Why do you ask?

 Kurt: I'm having lunch with a friend at Istanbul Kitchen tomorrow.

 Jing: Oh, you'll like it. I ⁴ _____ (**eat**) there several times.

3 **Shane:** We need another player for our volleyball team.

 Layla: ⁵ _____ you _____ (**see**) Chris play before? I heard he's good.

 Shane: Yeah. I ⁶ _____ (**watch**) him play last year. He's not bad.

 Layla: Why don't you ask him if he wants to try out?

E **Work in groups.** Write three true and three false sentences about things you have done. Read out your sentences. The others guess which ones are false.

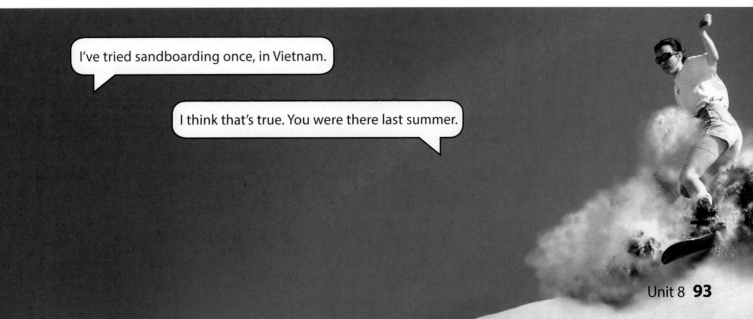

I've tried sandboarding once, in Vietnam.

I think that's true. You were there last summer.

LANTERN *FESTIVAL*

People from around the world release lanterns during the Yi Peng festival in Thailand.

A ▶ 8.1 **Watch the video.** Circle **T** for True or **F** for False.

1 The Yi Peng Festival is the biggest lantern festival in Thailand. **T** **F**

2 The festival happens in September every year. **T** **F**

3 People believe that releasing the lanterns brings good luck. **T** **F**

B ▶ 8.1 **Watch again.** Circle the correct answers.

1 The Yi Peng Festival takes place in the city of **Bangkok / Chiang Mai**.

2 The festival takes place when the **moon is full / rainy season ends**.

3 People decorate their lanterns with **pictures / wishes**.

4 They wait for the **wind / hot air** to carry their lanterns up into the sky.

DO YOU KNOW?

The La Tomatina festival in Spain is the world's largest

_____.

a eating contest
b festival
c food fight

C **Work with a partner.** How else do people make wishes around the world? Complete the sentences with words from the box. Then guess which countries the traditions come from.

> boats   coins   feathers   paper

1 People throw _____ into a fountain.   ○   ○   India

2 People fold 1,000 _____ birds to get a wish.   ○   ○   Italy

3 People float tiny _____ made of leaves down a river.   ○   ○   Japan

4 Children hide peacock _____ in books.   ○   ○   Thailand

D   CRITICAL THINKING Personalizing   **Talk with a partner.** Imagine you're at the Yi Peng Festival. What wishes would you write on your lantern? Think of three things.

> **PROJECT Find out more about a festival.** Choose one that you have never been to. Answer these questions:
>
> What is it called?   Where does it take place?
> When does it happen?   How do people celebrate it?

PRONUNCIATION reduction of *been*

🎧 8.5 **Listen**. Write the missing words. Then listen again and repeat the sentences.

1 I've never _____ New Zealand.

2 Have you ever _____ TV?

3 I've _____ Bangkok for two years.

4 I've _____ twice before.

COMMUNICATION

Work in groups. List three memorable experiences. Find two people who have done each thing in your list or something similar. Write down any additional information.

Memorable Experiences	Names	Additional Information
1 I've _____		
2 I've _____		
3 I've _____		

> Have you ever participated in a talent show?

> No, I haven't. But I've performed on TV before.

Jack Reynolds, age 105, rides a roller coaster in North Yorkshire, UK.

READING

A **Predict.** Look at the popular bucket list items on the right. A bucket list is a list of _____.

   a dangerous and challenging activities

   b activities people can do while traveling

   c things people want to do before they die

B **Scan the first three paragraphs.** What examples of bucket list items can you find?

C **Talk with a partner.** Choose one item in **B** to put on your own bucket list.

BUCKET
L I S T S

🎧 **8.6** Have you ever wanted to see the Great Wall of China, win an Oscar, or swim with dolphins? If so, you're not alone.

We all have things we want to do in our **lifetimes**.
5 Write those things down, and you have your very own bucket list. A bucket list is a list of things someone wants to experience before dying. It's **essentially** a set of goals that people create to **remind** themselves to live life to the fullest.

10 Many people have fun or exciting activities on their bucket lists, like hot-air ballooning or scuba diving. Others include places or things they want to see, like the Taj Mahal or the northern lights. Some people list things they want to achieve, like learning
15 a new language or completing a marathon. And others list things that are **worthwhile** and that make a positive difference in the world.

Laura Lawson is only 23, but she has already done half of the 333 items on her bucket list. She's eaten
20 an insect, visited Las Vegas, and gone skydiving. Her advice is simple: "Try not watching TV for a week. You'll see how much time you have to suddenly try new things."

Jack Reynolds shows that age is not a limit when it
25 comes to bucket lists. At 104, he flew in a biplane. And at 105, he became the world's oldest roller coaster passenger. For his 106th birthday, Jack wanted to ride in a Formula 1 car, but couldn't. So he went zip-lining instead!

30 Bucket lists are very **personal**. And the items on them don't have to be expensive to be worth doing. The best bucket lists **balance** experiencing the world, trying new things, and finding yourself. So think about what you enjoy, and ask yourself:

35 What's on your bucket list?

POPULAR BUCKET LIST ITEMS

- swim with dolphins
- learn a new language
- do volunteer work
- get a Ph.D.
- see Venice
- adopt a rescue dog
- go skydiving
- visit Machu Picchu
- learn to paint

COMPREHENSION

A Answer the questions about *Bucket Lists.*

1 VOCABULARY What's another way to say *live life to the fullest* (line 9)?

   a put one goal before all others

   b learn from past experiences

   c make the best use of your time

2 PURPOSE What is the purpose of the third paragraph?

   a to describe different types of bucket list items

   b to list the most popular bucket list items

   c to suggest the best types of bucket list items

3 INFERENCE Which statement would Laura Lawson probably agree with most?

   a Bucket lists take up a lot of time.

   b People should watch more TV.

   c You have more time than you think.

4 DETAIL According to the article, which of these things has Jack Reynolds done?

   a gone skydiving   b driven a Formula 1 car   c set a world record

5 DETAIL According to the article, the best bucket lists _____.

   a allow you to make new friends

   b include goals that are expensive

   c help you learn about yourself

B Read the third paragraph again. It describes four types of bucket list items. Then look at the nine "Popular Bucket List Items" on the previous page. Put each item in the correct column.

fun or exciting activities	places or things to see	things people want to achieve	activities that make a difference

C CRITICAL THINKING Applying Work in groups. What's on your bucket list? Which items are the easiest to achieve, and which are the hardest? Which require the most time?

VOCABULARY

A **Find the words below in the article.** Then circle the correct answers.

1 A **lifetime** refers to *when someone was born / the period someone is alive.*

2 You use **essentially** to *state a main idea / suggest a different idea.*

3 You **remind** someone about something to help them *remember / understand.*

4 If something is **worthwhile**, it is a *good / bad* thing to do.

5 If you say something is **personal**, it's about *you / everyone.*

6 If you **balance** two or more things, you give them *equal / greater* importance.

B **Read the information below.** Then write the words in the correct column to make phrases.

> A collocation is made up of two or more words that naturally go together. For example:
>
> We say **go** skydiving, NOT **play** skydiving.
>
> We say **take** a break, NOT **make** a break.

| ballet | a class | golf | a photo |
| professional soccer | something worthwhile | traveling | windsurfing |

do + _____	*take* + _____	*play* + _____	*go* + _____

WRITING

A **Read the online forum post.**

B **What memorable experiences have you had?** Think of three events and why they were memorable. Make notes.

C **Write your own response to the online forum question.**

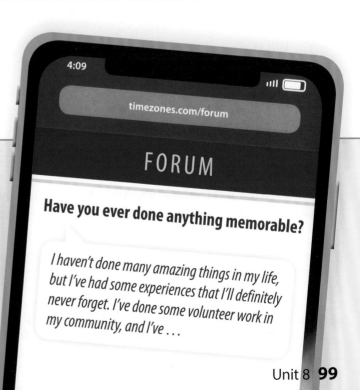

4:09

timezones.com/forum

FORUM

Have you ever done anything memorable?

I haven't done many amazing things in my life, but I've had some experiences that I'll definitely never forget. I've done some volunteer work in my community, and I've . . .

SAILING SOLO

Before You Watch

Take a quiz. Read the passage and circle the correct options. What else do you know about this part of the world?

French Polynesia is located in the [1] **Pacific / Atlantic** Ocean, halfway between South America and [2] **Australia / Africa**. It is made up of [3] **8 / 118** islands. The two largest islands are [4] **Hawaii / Tahiti** and Hiva Oa. French Polynesia is famous for its blue waters and perfect beaches.

While You Watch

A   ▶ 8.2 **Watch the video.** Check (✓) five things you see Laura doing.

- ☐ sailing
- ☐ fishing
- ☐ hiking
- ☐ climbing rocks
- ☐ cycling
- ☐ surfing
- ☐ swimming
- ☐ walking on a beach

B   ▶ 8.2 **Watch again.** Circle the correct answers.

1 Laura started her trip from _____ .

  a Gibraltar   **b** French Polynesia

2 She followed the route her parents took _____ .

  a a year ago   **b** over 20 years ago

3 Laura went to French Polynesia because she _____ .

  a saw her parents' photos   **b** read her father's diary

C **What does Laura think?** Match the parts of the sentences.

1 The culture on every island is	○ ○	the most important thing.
2 The people on the islands are	○ ○	amazing.
3 People back home are	○ ○	different.
4 Money is not	○ ○	too busy.

After You Watch

Talk with a partner. Laura thinks the Pacific islands are paradise. Why do you think she feels this way? What would you describe as paradise?

A Complete the activities. Use the words in the box.

> ballooning   boarding   diving   jumping
> karting   lining   riding   sailing

1 sand _____

2 go- _____

3 sky _____

4 para _____

5 bungee _____

6 zip-_____

7 hot-air _____

8 horseback _____

B Complete the conversations. Use the correct form of the verbs in parentheses.

1 **A:** [1]_____ you _____ Brazilian food? (**ever have**)

   B: Yes. I [2]_____ it last year. (**try**)

2 **C:** [3]_____ Jason _____ kitesurfing? (**ever go**)

   D: No, but his brother [4]_____ it many times. (**do**)

3 **E:** Jennifer says she [5]_____ camping. (**never be**)

   F: Neither have I. But I [6]_____ hiking last summer. (**go**)

Laura Dekker and her 12-meter-long sailboat, *Guppy*

www.lauradekker.nl

C Circle the correct words to make collocations.

1 My cousin has **done** / **played** soccer for his country.

2 I would like to **go** / **do** traveling after I graduate.

4 You can't **do** / **take** photos in the museum.

3 Have you ever **played** / **gone** windsurfing? It looks fun!

5 She's **done** / **gone** many worthwhile things in her life.

6 Have you ever **taken** / **gone** a cooking class?

SELF CHECK   Now I can …

☐ talk about interesting people and what they've done

☐ use language for talking about life experiences

☐ discuss what I want to achieve in my lifetime

PHONES USED TO BE MUCH **BIGGER!**

PREVIEW

A 🎧 9.1 **Listen.** Complete the sentences using the words in the box.

call	chat online	email	write letters	uses social media	sends texts

1 Kyle's parents used to _____, but now they _____. ○   ○ It's friendlier.

2 Deena used to _____, but now she _____. ○   ○ It's quick and easy.

3 Sofia used to _____, but now she _____. ○   ○ Everyone uses it.

A man talks on a cell phone in Shenzhen, China, 1993.

SCIENCE AND TECHNOLOGY

UNIT GOALS

- talk about things that have changed in your life

- learn to describe how things used to be

- find out about old technologies and gadgets

B 🎧 9.1 **Listen again.** Match the people to the reason for their preference.

C **Talk with a partner.** How do you like to communicate? Why? Which ways of communicating don't you like?

I like to text. It's quick and easy. I don't like email.

LANGUAGE FOCUS

A 🎧 **9.2** **Listen and read.** What was Stig's old phone like? Then repeat the conversation and replace the words in **bold**.

Stig: Hey, Maya. Check out my new phone!

Maya: Wow! That's a good phone! It used to be really expensive, right? Is it cheaper now?

Stig: Yes, it is. It's such an amazing phone. It's light, and it's really fast, too. My old phone **was so slow**. (**froze all the time** / **took forever to charge**)

Maya: Does it take good photos? You used to take **terrible** pictures with your old phone! (**horrible** / **awful**)

Stig: Yeah, it does. It has a fantastic camera.

Maya: Cool! Let's take a selfie together.

Stig: Sure. Give me a second. Hmm …

Maya: **What's wrong**? (**What's the matter** / **Is something wrong**)

Stig: Err … **I don't know how to unlock it!** (**I can't remember my password** / **The thumbprint reader isn't working**)

B 🎧 **9.3** **Look at the chart.** Circle the correct words to complete the sentences below.

DESCRIBING PAST STATES AND ACTIVITIES (USING *USED TO*)	
States	Phones **used to be** much bigger in the past. This phone didn't **use to cost** so much.
Activities	My mother **used to write** me letters, but now she emails. When I was young, I **never used to shop** online. Now I do it all the time.
Questions	**Did** she **use to** send you emails? **Did** your grandfather **use to** call you every day?

1 When we say *used to*, the past activity is **still** / **no longer** happening now.

2 One way to make *used to* negative is *did not* + **use to** / **used to**.

3 When asking questions, we say *Did she* **use to** / **used to**.

C 🎧 9.4 **Complete the conversations.** Use the correct form of *used to* and the words in parentheses. Then listen and check your answers.

1 Susan: Look at these old records! Are they yours?

    Paulo: No, they're my father's. He [1] _____ (**collect**) them when he was younger.

    Susan: Does he still play them?

    Paulo: No. He [2] _____ (**play**) them after dinner sometimes, but not anymore. We don't even have a record player now.

2 Terry: [3] _____ you _____ (**live**) in Montreal with your sister?

    Caitlin: Yes, I did. But I moved away three years ago.

    Terry: Oh. Do you still talk to her much?

    Caitlin: We video chat a lot. I [4] _____ (**never / like**) video chatting, but now I love it. Back in Montreal, we [5] _____ (**see**) each other just once a week. Now, we video chat all the time!

D Write sentences about things in your life that have changed. Then discuss what you wrote with a partner. Which changes are good, and which are bad?

1 _There used to be a bookstore near my house, but now it's gone._

2 _____

3 _____

4 _____

5 _____

E Work with a partner. Student A: Turn to page 152. **Student B:** Turn to page 154. You are going to compare two pictures of someone.

A collection of old vinyl records

A family plays *Space Invaders* on an Atari gaming console in 1978.

CLASSIC VIDEO GAMES

A ▶9.1 **Guess the answers.** Match the games to the descriptions. Then watch the video and check your answers.

1 *Pong* ○ ○ A fighter jet protects Earth from attacking aliens.
2 *Space Invaders* ○ ○ Two brothers try to rescue a princess from a monster.
3 *Super Mario Bros.* ○ ○ Two players hit a ball back and forth until one misses.

B ▶9.1 **Watch again.** Match the information (**a–f**) and the games (**1–3**).

a sold 40 million copies
b became popular in the late 1970s
c started the video game industry
d inspired a TV series and a movie
e early machines couldn't hold all the coins
f some believed it caused coin shortages

1 *Pong* _____

2 *Space Invaders* _____

3 *Super Mario Bros.* _____

C **Work with a partner.** Read the game review on the next page. Then match the headings below with the sentences.

Graphics   Difficulty Level   Level of Fun   Music   Story

GAME REVIEW

Hi, everyone! Last week, I finished playing the latest *Final Fantasy*. Here's my review. ★ ★ ★ ★ ☆

1 _____ The writing was excellent and included some clever twists and turns.

2 _____ Overall, the visuals were amazing. The characters and places looked great!

3 _____ The soundtrack really suited the mood of the game.

4 _____ The game was challenging, but stage 4 was nearly impossible. I almost gave up!

5 _____ The beginning was a little boring, but it gets really enjoyable after stage 2. You'll love it!

D **CRITICAL THINKING Applying** **Talk with a partner.** Choose a modern video game that you think will become a classic someday. What do you think makes it special?

PROJECT Research a classic video game. If possible, play it online. Write a short review. Use the five categories in **C** and give the game a "star" rating.

PRONUNCIATION reduction of *used to*

🎧 9.5 **Listen.** Complete the sentences. Then listen again and repeat the sentences.

1 Computers _____ so expensive.

2 Students didn't _____ their textbooks online.

3 Laptops _____ DVD drives.

4 People didn't _____ on their phones in restaurants.

COMMUNICATION

A **Write about yourself.** Write three surprising or embarrassing things that used to be true on three pieces of paper. Don't write your name!

> I used to have a collection of stuffed snakes.

> I used to sleep with the lights on because I was afraid of the dark.

> I used to practice walking like a model in front of my mirror.

B **Work in groups.** Mix your pieces of paper together and take three new pieces of paper. Ask questions to find out who wrote each sentence.

> Did you use to practice taking selfies in your room?

> No, I didn't. Did you use to wear a Hello Kitty headband?

READING

A **Work with a partner.** What do you see in the photos? Have you ever used any of these things?

B **Skim the article.** Then label the paragraphs with the headings below. One heading is extra.

Goodbye Disks   Music to My Ears
Picture This   Call Me Anytime

C **Scan the article.** Underline the tech items. Which ones can you find in the photos?

People used to use these items all the time.

THE THINGS WE USED *TO DO*

A 🎧9.6 Improvements in technology often happen overnight. Some gadgets get smaller and faster. Others are **replaced** by newer **devices** like smartphones, which can now do hundreds of things. Here are some old gadgets that people used to use.

1 _____

B Do you have a landline at home? These are phones that people plug into their living room walls. Cell phones didn't use to be so common, so most families had a landline. This is often no longer the case—not when each person in the family has their own cell phone. But landlines only worked at home. What did people do when they were outside and needed to call someone? They searched their pockets for coins and looked for a pay phone!

2 _____

C People today **store** large amounts of information online, or on flash drives or SD cards. But in the 1980s and 1990s, people used to use floppy disks. The first floppy disks were eight-inch-wide squares. They were **enormous**, expensive, and not very useful—each disk could store just 175 KB of information! Later, floppy disks got smaller and better. But even the best ones could only hold 1.44 MB. You would need three or four disks just for one song, and about 22,000 disks to match the storage **available** on a 32 GB phone!

3 _____

D It's easy to take photographs today. People often have thousands just on their phones! But before cameras went digital, photographs used to be expensive, and people took far fewer of them. To take a photo, you had to buy a roll of film. This allowed you to take about 20 or 30 photographs. After finishing the roll, you left it at a store. The store developed the photos, which you could only collect after a few days.

E Technology changes all the time, and the devices we use today will one day be old. What do you think will be next to **disappear**?

COMPREHENSION

A **Answer the questions about** *The Things We Used To Do.*

1 MAIN IDEA Choose another title for this article.

   a Technology Then and Now

   b The Gadgets of Tomorrow

   c How Smartphones Changed the World

2 DETAIL According to the article, which is true?

   a Landlines are still popular with older people.

   b Many homes today no longer have landlines.

   c Landlines died out because they became too expensive.

3 DETAIL What is NOT mentioned as a drawback to floppy disks?

   a They broke easily.   **b** They cost a lot.   **c** They were very big.

4 VOCABULARY In paragraph D, what does *before cameras went digital* mean?

   a before they became smaller and better

   b before they used computer technology

   c before they became popular

5 COHESION Where is the best place for this sentence in paragraph D?

"But not before paying to get the film developed."

   a after the second sentence   **b** after the fourth sentence   **c** after the last sentence

B **Read the statements.** Check (✓) the ones you can infer to be true from the reading.

  ☐ Most people in a home shared a landline.

  ☐ For a time, many people had pay phones in their homes.

  ☐ Most people used floppy disks to store music.

  ☐ The biggest problem with floppy disks was that they couldn't store much.

  ☐ People used to be more careful when taking photos.

  ☐ Some people developed their own photos at home.

C CRITICAL THINKING Analyzing **Talk with a partner.** The reading says that smartphones can now do hundreds of things. What are three things modern phones can do? How did people use to do these things?

DO YOU KNOW?

The first handheld cell phone _____.
a weighed four kilograms
b took two days to charge
c cost $4,000

VOCABULARY

A **Find the words below in the article.** Then complete the passage.
Use the correct form of the words in the box.

replace	device	store
enormous	available	disappear

IDIOM

If something
"happens overnight,"
it happens _____.
a in the evening
b suddenly
c too late

In 2001, Apple developed a(n) ¹ _____ that changed the
way people listened to music. The iPod wasn't the first MP3 player,
but unlike many others, it could ² _____ a lot of songs—1,000
in fact, which was a(n) ³ _____ number at the time. As soon as the iPod became
⁴ _____ in stores, it sold quickly. The iPod was so successful that MP3s soon
⁵ _____ CDs! CD players ⁶ _____ , and MP3 players took over.

B **Read the information below.** Then complete the sentences with the expressions in the box.

> Computers allow us to *store* huge amounts of data. Here are some
> other common tasks we do on computers.
>
> *back up*: make an extra copy of something
>
> *delete*: remove something from a computer
>
> *download*: get files from the internet
>
> *save*: store something on a computer or storage device

1 If you don't need these files, _____ them. They take up too much space.

2 It's taking a long time to _____ the videos from this website.

3 Don't forget to _____ the changes you make to the presentation.

4 I always _____ the files on my computer—I keep copies on my flash drive.

WRITING

A **Read the blog post.**

B **Think of a gadget that you used to have.** What did it do? How did you use it? Make notes.

C **Write a blog post about the gadget.** Include a photo of the gadget.

When I was young, I had an Xbox 360. I used to play video games on it all the time. I also used it to play DVDs ...

CREATING THE *INTERNET*

Before You Watch

Talk with a partner. How much time do you spend online a day? How do you feel when you don't have access to the internet?

While You Watch

A   ▶ 9.2   **Watch the video.** Circle **T** for True or **F** for False.

1 Today, over 4 billion people have access to the internet.   **T**   **F**

2 The internet began in the United States.   **T**   **F**

3 The first computer networks connected different organizations.   **T**   **F**

4 ARPANET was an early version of the internet.   **T**   **F**

5 The internet became popular with regular people in the 1980s.   **T**   **F**

B   ▶ 9.2   **Watch again.** Then number the events in order (1–5) to summarize the history of the internet.

_____ The internet covers the whole world.

___1___ Small computer networks connect computers within organizations.

_____ ARPANET grows and includes many government and research organizations.

_____ Personal computers start becoming popular.

_____ The U.S. Department of Defense connects different organizations' networks.

C   **Look at the four items.** The video says that all sorts of devices now make use of the internet. How has the internet made these items better?

1 doorbell   ○   ○ You can keep the house clean while on vacation.
2 refrigerator   ○   ○ You can set the temperature before you get home.
3 air conditioner   ○   ○ You can see who's there even when you're not at home.
4 vacuum cleaner   ○   ○ You can use cameras to check how much food you have left.

After You Watch

Talk with a partner. According to the video, "Few technological innovations have made as great an impact as the internet." Do you agree? What did people do differently before the internet?

A Complete the sentences. Use the words in the box.

> chat   device   digital   graphics   social media   text

1 He likes to see what his friends are up to on _____ .

2 I like to _____ with my friends online or on my phone.

3 Don't call me later. Just send me a _____ .

4 This game looks great. The _____ are amazing!

5 Before _____ cameras, people had to use film.

6 That phone is an amazing _____ .

B Write sentences or questions. Use *used to.*

1 I / have / three laptops

_____ .

2 you / live / in New York

_____ ?

3 he / not / enjoy / video games

_____ .

4 there / never / be / a bookstore here

_____ .

C Circle the correct answers.

1 Floppy disks didn't use to **store** / **delete** much information.

2 I **backed up** / **downloaded** the video from that website.

3 I accidentally **deleted** / **saved** the file. Do you have a copy?

4 Can I **save** / **store** this document to your flash drive?

5 Try to **download** / **back up** your files often, in case your computer crashes.

The internet has come a long way since its early days.

SELF CHECK   Now I can …

☐ talk about things that have changed in my life

☐ describe how things used to be

☐ discuss old technologies and gadgets

THEY'VE MADE AN
AMAZING
DISCOVERY!

Scotty's fossil at the T.rex Discovery Centre in Canada

PREVIEW

A 🎧 10.1 **Listen to the news stories.** Number the titles in order (1–3). One title is extra.

_____ A Return to Sight

_____ An Accidental Discovery

_____ Swimming With Rats

_____ King of the Dinosaurs

B 🎧 10.1 **Listen again.** Complete the sentences using the words in the box.

> messages fossil shapes rat *T. rex* tree

1 Researchers in Canada have identified the heaviest _____ ever found. They first discovered its _____ back in 1991.

2 Scientists in the Solomon Islands have discovered a giant _____. They found it after it fell from a _____.

3 Four blind patients have received "bionic eyes" that allow them to see _____. The eyes use cameras and sensors to send _____ to the brain.

C **Work with a partner.** Choose one story and retell it. Include as many details as possible.

> Researchers in Canada have found a *T. rex* fossil. They believe …

HISTORY AND CULTURE

UNIT GOALS

• talk about things that happened to you recently

• learn how to describe recently completed actions

• find out about some interesting recent discoveries

LANGUAGE FOCUS

A 🎧 **10.2 Listen and read.** Where is Nadine going? Then repeat the conversation and replace the words in **bold**.

Maya:	Guess what. I've just **joined** the Dinosaur Club! (**signed up for** / **become a member of**)
Nadine:	Cool! I've been a member **since last year**! (**for a year** / **since it started**)
Maya:	I know! So what do you do at the Dinosaur Club? Go to museums?
Nadine:	This week will be special. Researchers have **found** some fossils in the desert. We're going to help look for more! (**discovered** / **come across**)
Maya:	Oh … wow. The desert? That sounds … **interesting**. (**challenging** / **hot**)
Nadine:	I know! I can't wait. I've already packed my sunscreen. Imagine if we find something!
Maya:	Yeah … You know, maybe the Dinosaur Club isn't for me.

B 🎧 **10.3 Look at the chart.** Read the sentences below. Circle **T** for True or **F** for False.

DESCRIBING PAST ACTIONS (USING SIMPLE PAST AND PRESENT PERFECT)	
Simple past	**Present perfect**
I **applied** for membership last week.	I've (just) **gotten** my membership card.
They **arrived at the hotel** three hours ago.	They've (just) **gone** to the museum.
Where **did** she **go**? She **went** to the lab.	Where **has** she **gone**? She's **gone** to the lab.
Duration of continuing actions	
How long have you been a member?	I've **been** a member **for** a year.
	I've **been** a member **since** last year.

1 We can use the present perfect to discuss things that have just happened.   **T**   **F**

2 We use *for* + a point in time (e.g., *last week* or *last month*).   **T**   **F**

3 We use *since* + a length of time (e.g., *a year* or *two months*).   **T**   **F**

C 🎧 **10.4 Complete the conversations.** Circle the correct answers. Then listen and check.

1 **Leena:** Hey, Michael. ¹ **Did you watch / Have you watched** the news last night?

Michael: No, I ² **was / have been** at the library until late. What happened?

Leena: Well, there ³ **was / has been** an interesting story about a group of children. They ⁴ **found / have found** some dinosaur fossils a few days ago!

2 **Tyler:** I'm so sorry, Soo-jin. My train ⁵ **was / has been** late. How long ⁶ **were you / have you been** here?

Soo-jin: Not long. I ⁷ **arrived / have arrived** about five minutes ago.

Tyler: That's good. So where do you want to go? How about Canyon Café?

Soo-jin: No, thanks. I ⁸ **went / have gone** there last week. Let's go somewhere else.

3 **Jennie:** I've just ⁹ **saw / seen** my chemistry test score. Another C.

Raul: That's not so bad for chemistry, is it?

Jennie: Well, last year I ¹⁰ **had / have had** mostly Bs. I think I need a tutor.

Raul: How about Sarah? She ¹¹ **scored / has scored** really well on her chemistry test.

D **Complete the sentences.** Write *for* or *since*.

1 I've been part of the research team _____ seven months.

2 The museum has had the bones on display _____ 1998.

3 Researchers haven't found any fossils there _____ last year.

4 Aisha has been a member of the Science Club _____ two years.

5 Raul has been studying nonstop _____ three weeks!

6 Li Ling hasn't texted me _____ she left for her vacation.

E **Work with a partner. Student A:** Turn to page 153. **Student B:** Turn to page 155. Ask and answer questions to complete the missing information.

A meteorite falling over Whitby, England

LIGHTS IN THE SKY

An aurora
lights up the
night sky in Norway.

A Work with a partner. How do auroras form? Label the diagram with the sentences (**a–d**).

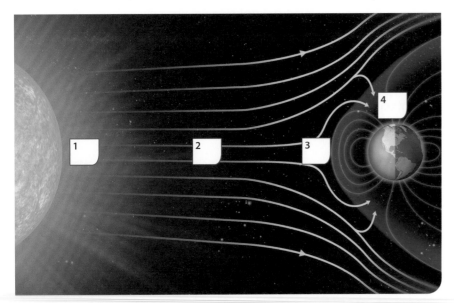

a Solar winds move toward Earth.

b A solar flare shoots out from the sun.

c Solar winds come together near the Earth's poles. Auroras appear.

d Solar winds hit Earth's magnetic field.

B ▶ 10.1 **Watch the video.** Circle the correct answer.

Scientists / Amateur astronomers were the ones who first discovered STEVEs.

C ▶ 10.1 **Watch again.** What does the video say about STEVEs?

1 STEVEs are **green and yellow** / **purple** lights in the sky.

2 STEVEs are **long thin lines** / **spread out**.

3 STEVEs point **north to south** / **east to west**.

4 STEVEs occur **higher up** / **lower down** than regular auroras.

5 Scientists **know** / **don't know** what causes STEVEs.

D **CRITICAL THINKING Justifying** **Talk with a partner.** Amateur astronomers created the nickname STEVE, but scientists later made the name official. Is STEVE a good name? Why or why not?

PROJECT Where can you go to see auroras? Find out the best places to view them. Which spot would you like to visit the most?

PRONUNCIATION reduction of *has* and *have*

🎧 10.5 **Listen.** Write the words you hear. Then listen again and repeat the sentences.

1 _____ found some interesting rocks in the area.

2 Our _____ given us a big project to do.

3 Why _____ kept the discovery a secret?

4 What _____ discovered about the new type of aurora?

COMMUNICATION

A **Work in groups.** Choose a photo about a recent discovery. Prepare to give a short news conference. Answer the questions below using your own ideas.

Who made the discovery? **When** did they discover it?

Where did they discover it? **Why** is the discovery important?

B **Take turns reporting your story.** The other students in your group are journalists. Answer their questions.

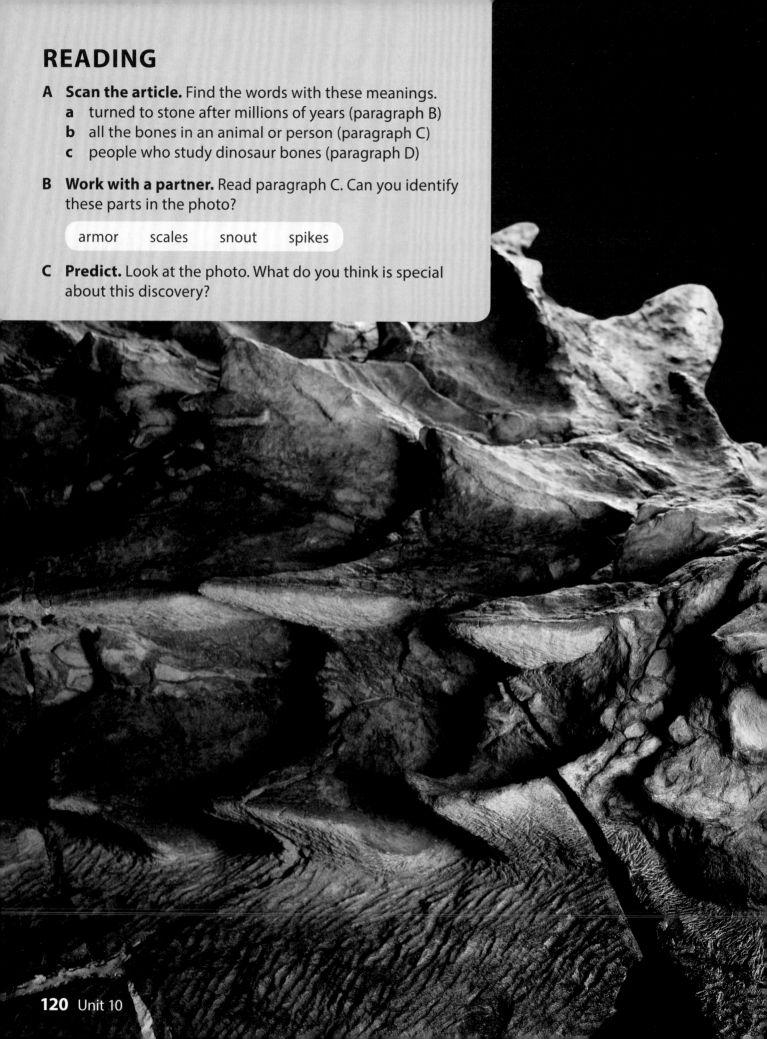

READING

A **Scan the article.** Find the words with these meanings.
   a turned to stone after millions of years (paragraph B)
   b all the bones in an animal or person (paragraph C)
   c people who study dinosaur bones (paragraph D)

B **Work with a partner.** Read paragraph C. Can you identify these parts in the photo?

   armor   scales   snout   spikes

C **Predict.** Look at the photo. What do you think is special about this discovery?

TURNED
TO STONE

A 🎧 10.6 Workers in Canada have made an exciting discovery. Machine operator Shawn Funk was digging through the earth when he noticed something much harder than the rock around it. "It was definitely nothing we had ever seen before," said Funk.

B A local museum now displays Funk's discovery. It looks like a piece of art, but it's not. It's a fossilized dinosaur—one of the most amazing ever found!

C After 110 million years underground, it has turned to stone, from its snout to its hips. Armor covers its neck and back. Two 50-centimeter spikes stick out from its shoulders. Fossilized skin and scales cover its body. Caleb Brown, a researcher at the museum, is amazed by the quality of the fossil. "We don't just have a skeleton. We have a dinosaur as it would have been."

D For paleontologists, a find like this is very rare. Usually, only the bones and teeth are preserved—softer parts like the skin and scales rarely get fossilized. The dinosaur is so well preserved it even has a little bit of its original color. But why is this dinosaur fossil so different? Scientists have a theory.

E They think that the dinosaur's carcass was carried into a river by a flood. It reached the sea, and after a week or so, the carcass sank to the ocean floor. Mud covered it and entered its skin, armor, and bones. After millions of years, this made the creature's body stonelike.

F Scientists have studied the fossil carefully, but it will take years to learn all its secrets. Its bones, for example, are under its skin and armor, and paleontologists need to find a way to reach them without destroying its body. In some ways, this dinosaur is almost too well preserved!

This nodosaur fossil is about 110 million years old.

COMPREHENSION

A Answer the questions about *Turned to Stone*.

1 **DETAIL** Shawn Funk _____.

   a found the fossil by accident

   b worked as a paleontologist

   c was digging for dinosaur bones

2 **INFERENCE** Why does the author say the dinosaur looks like a piece of art?

   a It is colorful.   b It is made of stone.   c It is well preserved.

3 **DETAIL** What makes this discovery different from other dinosaur discoveries?

   a It is 110 million years old.

   b Its bones and teeth are preserved.

   c Its skin and scales are fossilized.

4 **COHESION** Where is the best place for this sentence?

   "It also ensured that the dinosaur kept its shape."

   a the end of paragraph D

   b the end of paragraph E

   c the end of paragraph F

5 **INFERENCE** Why will it take years to fully study the fossil?

   a It is large and heavy.   b Its armor is very tough.   c Scientists don't want to damage it.

B Complete the flow chart. How did the dinosaur get fossilized? Use words from the reading.

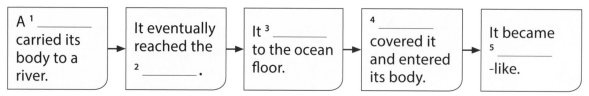

A ¹ _____ carried its body to a river. → It eventually reached the ² _____. → It ³ _____ to the ocean floor. → ⁴ _____ covered it and entered its body. → It became ⁵ _____ -like.

C CRITICAL THINKING Evaluating Talk with a partner. Why do scientists study dinosaurs? What questions do you think this fossil can help answer?

An illustration of a complete nodosaur

VOCABULARY

A **Find the words below in the article.** Then complete the sentences. Use the correct form of the words.

> quality   preserve   original   reach   secret   destroy

1 The storm completely _____ the house.

2 I asked her what Arnold said, but she told me it was a(n) _____ .

3 After months of sailing, the ship finally _____ Singapore.

4 This painting isn't the _____ . It's a copy.

5 People often _____ food by drying it in the sun.

6 These materials are cheaper, but their _____ is poor.

B **Read the information.** Then match the parts of the sentences to complete the job descriptions.

> The suffix *-logist* means "person who studies." We sometimes use it to make certain words for jobs.

1 A paleontologist ○   ○ studies old human-made objects.

2 An archaeologist ○   ○ studies how people think and act.

3 A biologist ○   ○ studies the Earth.

4 A psychologist ○   ○ studies plants and animals.

5 A geologist ○   ○ studies fossilized plants and animals.

WRITING

A **Read the news story.**

B **Choose a photo from the Communication activity on page 119.** Imagine the story behind the discovery. Use these questions to help you.

- *Who made the discovery?*   • *What did they discover?*
- *When did they find it?*   • *Where did they find it?*
- *How did they find it?*   • *Why is it important?*

C **Write a news story using your notes from B.**

DAILY NEWS

Mysterious Mask Found

Archaeologists in Egypt have found a 2,000-year-old mask in a cave near Giza. They believe it belonged to …

LINES IN THE SAND

Before You Watch

Look at the photo. What do you see in the drawings? How big do you think the drawings are?

While You Watch

A   ▶ 10.2   **Watch the video.** Check (✓) the drawings that are mentioned.

☐ a *tupu*   ☐ a bird   ☐ a fish

☐ a flying woman   ☐ a monkey   ☐ a tree

B   ▶ 10.2   **Watch again.** Choose the correct answers.

1   The drawings are about **1,000** / **2,000** years old.

2   Explorers first discovered the drawings **recently** / **a century ago**.

3   A *tupu* was a tool used to **cut pieces of cloth** / **hold clothing together**.

4   Explorers first realized what the drawings were after **planes** / **drones** were invented.

5   We can't see the drawings from the ground because they're **big** / **hard to find**.

C   **Read the sentences.** Then number the events in order (1–5).

_____ People invent airplanes.   _____ Archaeologists discover 50 new drawings.

_____ People invent drones.   _____ People see the drawings for the first time.

                                              __1__ People think the lines are roads.

After You Watch

Talk with a partner. What do you think the drawings mean, and why did people draw them? Come up with at least three theories.

A large drawing on a mountainside in Peru

A Complete the sentences. Use the words in the box.

| astronomer | discovery | fossil | quality | secret | skeleton |

1 Scientists have made an interesting _____ .

2 The _____ looked just like an actual dinosaur.

3 An amateur _____ first noticed the object in the sky.

4 He wasn't sure, so he kept his theory a(n) _____ .

5 The _____ of the student's work wasn't very good.

6 She found the complete _____ of a mammoth—not just a few bones.

B Circle the correct option. Are the sentences correct (✓) or incorrect (✗)?

1 My friends have just left for the museum.　✓　✗

2 Jose has arrived five minutes ago.　✓　✗

3 I'm not hungry. I've ate my dinner.　✓　✗

4 How long have you been an archaeologist?　✓　✗

5 She's gone to Australia to study for three years.　✓　✗

6 Priyanka has seen the movie last week.　✓　✗

C Complete the definitions. Write jobs ending with -logist.

1 A(n) _____ studies the Earth.

2 A(n) _____ studies plants and animals.

3 A(n) _____ studies how people think.

4 A(n) _____ studies fossilized animals.

5 A(n) _____ studies old human-made objects.

SELF CHECK　Now I can ...

☐ talk about things that happened to me recently

☐ use language for describing recently completed actions

☐ discuss interesting recent discoveries

BUY ONE, GET ONE
FREE!

BROADWAY

A large crowd gathers for a Black Friday sale in New York City, USA.

PREVIEW

A 🎧 **11.1 Listen to four advertisements.** What is each one selling? Number the pictures 1–4.

shampoo	mouthwash	deodorant	vitamins
___	___	___	___

B 🎧 **11.1 Listen again.** What does each advertisement say?

1 If you buy one, you'll **only pay 50%** / **get one free**.

2 If you download the app, you can **watch videos of the product** / **ask for a free sample**.

3 If you use it every day, your hair will be **stronger** / **straighter**.

4 If you use it regularly, your **teeth will be brighter** / **breath will be fresher**.

C **Talk with a partner.** Think of some memorable ads. What do you like or dislike about them?

> Have you seen that new burger ad that's on TV?

> The one with the cool song? It's really funny. I love it!

PEOPLE AND PLACES

UNIT GOALS

- talk about shopping and sales strategies
- learn language for talking about results
- discuss a new marketing trend

LANGUAGE FOCUS

A 🎧 **11.2 Listen and read.** What does Ming get if he buys a bottle of shampoo? Then repeat the conversation and replace the words in **bold**.

Ming: Have you ever **tried** this shampoo before? I saw an ad for it on TV the other night. (**bought** / **used**)

Stig: No, I haven't. Hmm. It says here that if you use it, your hair will be much **shinier** after just one week. (**stronger** / **smoother**)

Ming: That sounds good.

Stig: And look! If you buy a bottle, you'll get **another one free**. (**50% off the next one** / **a free bottle of conditioner**)

Ming: What a deal! I'm getting a bottle.

Stig: Hey Ming. It's been a week. How's the new shampoo?

Ming: Um … I think I'll **stick to** my old brand! (**go back to** / **continue to use**)

B 🎧 **11.3 Look at the chart.** Circle the correct answers below.

TALKING ABOUT RESULTS (USING FIRST CONDITIONALS)	
If you **buy** a bottle, you**'ll get** another one free.	
If you **download** our app, you **can ask** for a free sample.	
Your hair **will be** much shinier **if** you **use** this shampoo for a week.	
If you **use** it daily, you **won't have to worry** about bad breath.	
If you **aren't** happy, the store **will give** you your money back.	
If you **don't buy** it today, you **won't be able to buy** it later.	
If I buy three, **will** I get a discount?	Yes, you **will**. / No, you **won't**.
What **will** you **do if** the store **is** closed?	**I'll** go to another store.

1 Main clauses in first conditional statements describe **causes** / **results**.

2 The *if* clause **can** / **can't** be in the negative.

3 The main clause **can** / **can't** be in the negative.

C **Match the two parts to complete the sentences.**

1 If you don't have enough cash, ○   ○ you won't see any ads.
2 If you turn on the ad blocker, ○   ○ we'll enter your name in the prize draw.
3 If you complete this survey, ○   ○ you can pay with a credit card.
4 If you don't like your gift, ○   ○ the store will let you exchange it.

D 🎧 **11.4** **Read the advertisement.** Complete the passage using the correct form of the verbs. Listen and check.

GET YOURS TODAY!

If you ¹ _____ (**like**) to sing, you ² _____ (**love**) this. Introducing the Shower Microphone. It's a showerhead that looks just like a microphone! If you ³ _____ (**enjoy**) having fun, this ⁴ _____ (**keep**) you busy for hours. Sing as loud as you like— and keep clean while doing it! The cost? Only $9.95! And if you ⁵ _____ (**place**) an order today, there ⁶ _____ (**not be**) any shipping or handling charges. Plus, we ⁷ _____ (**include**) one extra Shower Microphone at no cost if you ⁸ _____ (**call**) in the next five minutes. So don't wait. Get your Shower Microphone today!

E **Work in groups.** Which of these things would you like to do? Choose three and discuss what you think will happen if each person does those things.

save more money	get a part-time job	learn to drive	quit social media
buy a new phone	exercise more	eat less junk food	watch less TV

SUPERMARKET TRICKS

This supermarket in London, UK is full of signs offering great deals.

A ▶ **11.1** **Watch the video.** Circle the correct answers.

1 Supermarkets put items that **cost more** / **smell nice** near the entrance.

2 Supermarkets also put **eggs and milk** / **fruit and vegetables** near the entrance.

3 Supermarkets put popular items at the **front** / **back** of the store.

4 Supermarkets put snacks near the **entrance** / **exit**.

B ▶ **11.1** **Watch again.** Label the diagram using the words in the box.

eggs   entrance   exit   snacks   vegetables

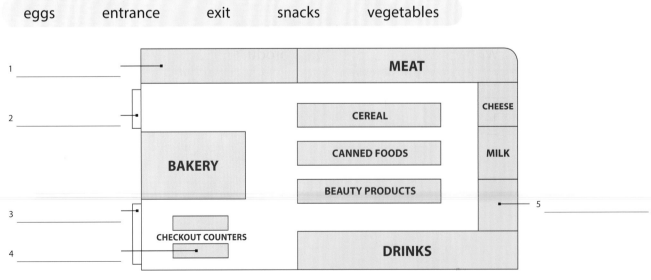

1 _____

2 _____

3 _____

4 _____

5 _____

MEAT

CEREAL

CANNED FOODS

BEAUTY PRODUCTS

CHEESE

MILK

BAKERY

CHECKOUT COUNTERS

DRINKS

C **Work with a partner.** Supermarkets use many other tricks to get customers to spend more. Match the two parts of the sentences.

1 If you put items at eye level, ○   ○ customers won't notice the time.

2 If you have larger shopping carts, ○   ○ customers will think they are fresher.

3 If you play slow music, ○   ○ more customers will notice them.

4 If you don't have windows, ○   ○ people will fill them up with more things.

5 If you splash water on vegetables, ○   ○ people will feel relaxed and shop more.

D (CRITICAL THINKING Ranking) **Talk with a partner.** Look at the tricks in **C**. How well do you think they work? Rank them from most (1) to least (5) effective.

PROJECT Choose a clothing or electronics store you know. If possible, visit it. Does it use the same tricks as the supermarket? What other tricks does it use?

PRONUNCIATION pauses after *if* clauses

🎧 **11.5 Listen.** Add a comma when you hear a pause. Then listen again and repeat the sentences.

1 If customers are happy they'll stay longer and buy more.

2 If you don't buy it today you won't be able to buy it later.

3 If you use it for one week your hair will be much stronger.

4 If you download our app you can ask for a free sample.

DO YOU KNOW?

Which item do US supermarkets sell the most of?
a bread
b chips
c soda

COMMUNICATION

A **Work with a partner.** Choose one of the products below. Think of a way to improve it.

toothpaste	running shoes	chewing gum	shampoo	coffee
headphones	an umbrella	a phone case	a straw	sunglasses

B **Work in groups.** With your partner, "pitch" your product by saying what it can do for you if you use it.

> Our product is amazing. It's a shampoo that colors your hair.

> If you use it, your hair will slowly change to a color of your choice!

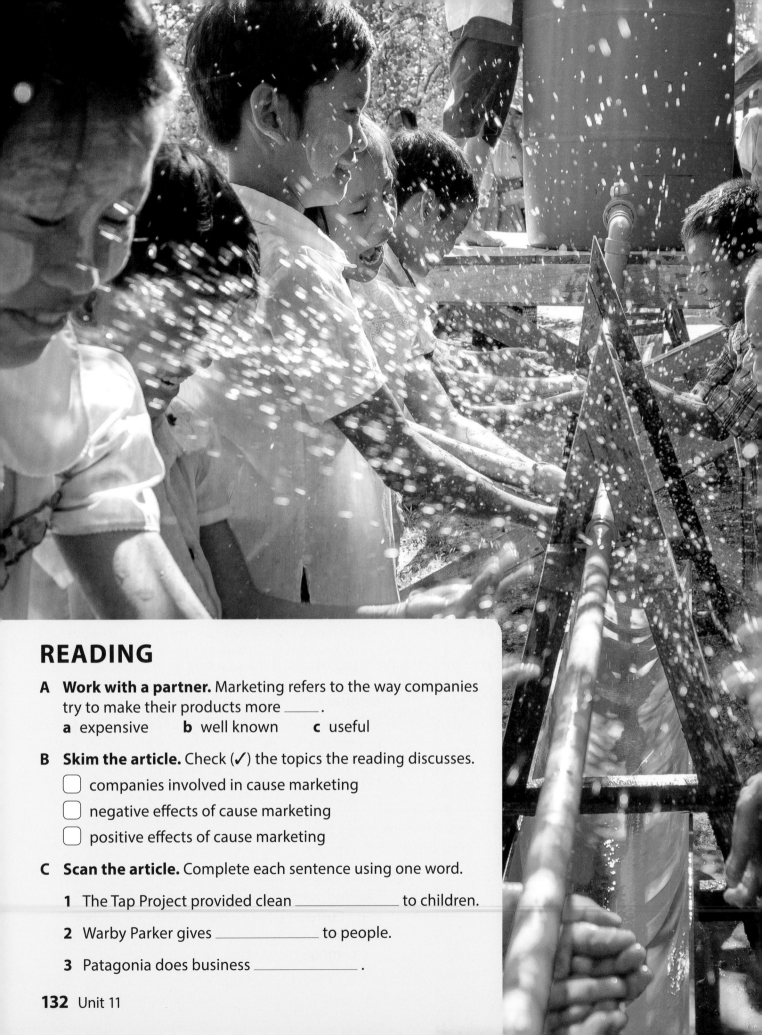

READING

A Work with a partner. Marketing refers to the way companies try to make their products more _____.

a expensive   **b** well known   **c** useful

B Skim the article. Check (✓) the topics the reading discusses.

☐ companies involved in cause marketing

☐ negative effects of cause marketing

☐ positive effects of cause marketing

C Scan the article. Complete each sentence using one word.

1 The Tap Project provided clean _____ to children.

2 Warby Parker gives _____ to people.

3 Patagonia does business _____ .

UNICEF helped provide clean drinking water to these children from Myanmar.

CAUSE MARKETING

🎧 11.6 You've probably heard of marketing. But what about cause marketing? These days, many customers prefer to buy from companies with good **values**. Cause marketing is a way for companies to
5 attract these customers and make money by doing good. Here are three examples:

The Tap Project

We all need clean drinking water, but not everyone can get it. The organization UNICEF came up with a
10 way to help. It got restaurant diners to **donate** a dollar for each glass of water they drank. It then used that money to help children around the world get clean water. The project made a huge difference. More than half a million people
15 **benefited**, and the number of people who got sick from drinking dirty water fell.

Buy a Pair, Give a Pair

Two and a half billion people around the world can't see clearly. Of these, over 600 million are unable to
20 work or study because they can't **afford** eyeglasses. The eyewear company Warby Parker is helping to reduce this number. If you buy a pair of glasses, it will donate another pair to someone who needs them. So far, Warby Parker has helped more than
25 5 million people get eyeglasses.

Business the Right Way

Many companies try to make money by using cheap materials, or by not paying their workers well. But some try to be more ethical. The clothes company
30 Patagonia uses only environmentally friendly materials in its products. It's also fair to its workers— it pays them well and gives them good benefits. Patagonia believes that if it does business ethically, people who **care** will notice and buy its products.

35 Cause marketing is a great way for companies to become more popular. It works because everybody wins. Customers get to buy what they want and help make a difference. People in need benefit. And the companies that take part get good **publicity**.

COMPREHENSION

A Answer the questions about *Cause Marketing*.

1 **VOCABULARY** The word *cause* in *cause marketing* means _____ .

   a a worthwhile goal

   b a difficult situation

   c a new way of thinking

2 **PURPOSE** The purpose of the reading is to _____ .

   a explain how companies can protect the environment

   b teach readers how to start a successful business

   c show how companies can make a difference

3 **DETAIL** What was the result of UNICEF's Tap Project?

   a customers at restaurants drank less water

   b people bought more bottled water

   c fewer people drank dirty water

4 **DETAIL** According to the article, Warby Parker _____ .

   a gives eyeglasses away   b asks for donations   c buys used eyeglasses

5 **INFERENCE** Which of these ideas would Patagonia probably NOT support?

   a using recycled materials to make their products

   b reducing break time so that workers produce more

   c paying its workers extra when they work longer hours

B Look at the actions below. Which brand does each action best match?

   a making sure its employees are not overworked
   b donating its products to places where people can't buy them
   c installing pipes in places where people don't have them
   d helping children to read so that they can complete their education
   e asking people to give money to help children around the world
   f avoiding products that damage the environment

1 The Tap Project   _____

2 Warby Parker   _____

3 Patagonia   _____

C CRITICAL THINKING Reflecting **Are a company's values important to you?** Are there companies you choose to buy from because of their values or practices? Are there companies you avoid?

VOCABULARY

A Find the words below in the article. Then complete the definitions using the words.

> values   donate   benefit   afford   care   publicity

1 When you _____ something, you give it to someone who needs it.

2 If you can _____ something, you have enough money to pay for it.

3 _____ refers to attention from a large number of people.

4 The ideas that help you decide right from wrong are your _____ .

5 You _____ from something if it leaves you in a better position than before.

6 If you _____ about something, it is important to you.

B Read the information below. Then complete the passage using the words in the box.

> *Marketing* and *publicity* are words that people often use in business. There are many other business words that people use, like the ones below.

> advertising   brand   profit   sales

Marketing involves many things. One of these things is
¹ _____ . Companies often pay to have their messages appear on TV, in magazines, or online. They want to get more publicity and make the company's
² _____ more famous. They believe that if the company's name is more well known,
³ _____ will increase. This will of course create more ⁴ _____ for the company.

Advertisements on buildings in Tokyo, Japan

WRITING

A Read the idea for a cause marketing campaign.

B Imagine you run a company. What product or service do you offer? Think of a good cause marketing campaign for your company. Make notes.

C Write a paragraph. Describe your cause marketing campaign.

People often get plastic lids for their coffee cups. My café will change that. If a customer refuses the plastic lid, my café will ...

GRAVITY STONES

Before You Watch

Complete the sentences. Use these words and a dictionary if necessary.

artificial	bias	gravity	scam	scarcity

1 If someone tricks you for money, you fell for a(n) _____ .

2 Things fall to the ground because of _____ .

3 If someone has a(n) _____ , they like one thing more than others.

4 A(n) _____ item isn't natural. It's human-made.

5 When there's not enough of something, there's a(n) _____ .

While You Watch

A ▶ 11.2 **Watch the video.** Circle **T** for True or **F** for False.

1	Each customer can only buy four stones.	T	F
2	Ben has been selling stones for many years.	T	F
3	The stones give you better balance.	T	F
4	If a salesperson looks good, more people will believe them.	T	F
5	The stones are very rare.	T	F

B ▶ 11.2 **Who says these things?** Write **S** (salesperson) or **C** (customer). Then watch the video and check your answers.

1 _____ These will change your life.

2 _____ I'm sold.

3 _____ I feel grounded.

4 _____ Suckers!

5 _____ That's amazing!

6 _____ There's real science in these.

7 _____ These are so rare.

8 _____ Today it's costing me $20.

C **Match the strategies to the examples.**

1 halo effect ○   ○ "He said it was the last jacket, so I quickly bought it."

2 expert bias ○   ○ "She was well dressed and smiled a lot. I felt I could trust her."

3 artificial scarcity ○   ○ "He had many years of experience, so I believed him."

After You Watch

Talk with a partner. What other types of scams have you heard of?

REVIEW

A Match the products to their descriptions.

1 toothpaste ○   ○ Use this to smell good all day.
2 deodorant ○   ○ Use every day to keep your hair shiny.
3 shampoo ○   ○ Brush twice a day so your teeth stay clean.
4 mouthwash ○   ○ Take one a day to stay healthy and strong.
5 vitamins ○   ○ Use after brushing for fresher breath.

B Complete the first conditional sentences.

1 If you _____ it, I _____ you another one free.
   (**buy**, **give**)

2 I _____ to another store if they _____ my
   favorite brand. (**go**, **not have**)

3 If I _____ you later, I _____ you tomorrow.
   (**not see**, **call**)

4 They _____ you a ticket if you _____ your
   passport. (**not give**, **not have**)

5 If he _____ late, _____ they _____
   him in? (**arrive**, **let**)

6 How _____ we _____ there if the weather is
   bad? (**get**)

C Circle the correct words.

1 The company plans to spend more on **profits** / **advertising**.

2 The new marketing campaign has led to increased **sales** / **brands**.

3 This deodorant isn't great. I prefer my old **advertising** / **brand**.

4 They increased their **profits** / **sales** by using cheaper materials.

SELF CHECK Now I can …

☐ discuss shopping and sales strategies

☐ use language for talking about results

☐ talk about a new marketing trend

WHICH PLANET IS THE BIGGEST?

sun

1

2

3

4

solar system

PREVIEW

A 🎧 12.1 **Listen.** Write the sentence that helps you remember the order of the planets.

_____

_____

B 🎧 12.1 **Listen.** Number the planets in order from 1 (closest to the sun) to 8 (farthest from the sun).

_____ Earth

_____ Mercury

_____ Uranus

_____ Jupiter

_____ Neptune

_____ Venus

_____ Mars

_____ Saturn

Our solar system is one of many
in the Milky Way galaxy.

planets

5

6

7

8

C **Talk with a partner.** Take turns asking and answering questions about our solar system.

Which planet is between Mercury and Earth?

It's Venus. Which planet has rings?

UNIT GOALS

- find out about space and our solar system

- use language for describing future activities

- learn about some important space discoveries

LANGUAGE FOCUS

A 🎧 **12.2 Listen and read.** What topic is Ming researching? Then repeat the conversation and replace the words in **bold**.

> **REAL ENGLISH** I have no idea.

Maya: Hey, Ming. What are you up to?

Ming: I'm doing some research. Our teacher gave us an assignment on **outer space**. (**space travel / our solar system**)

Maya: So what exactly are you doing for this assignment?

Ming: I'll be **making a poster** on astronauts, I think. (**preparing a presentation / writing an essay**)

Maya: Oh, that reminds me of a joke. Why didn't the astronaut **stay at the hotel on the moon**? (**eat at the moon's restaurant / have a birthday party**)

Ming: I have no idea.

Maya: Because **it was full**! (**it had no atmosphere / his friends forgot to planet**)

B 🎧 **12.3 Look at the chart.** Circle the correct words to complete the sentences below.

USING DIFFERENT TENSES		
Describing future activities	Future progressive	At 5 p.m. tomorrow, I**'ll be doing** my homework. This time next week, I**'ll be giving** a presentation.
Tense review	Present progressive Present perfect Future with *will* First conditional	I**'m doing** some research at the moment. I**'ve** (just) **finished** working on my space project. People **will** (probably) **live** on Mars someday. **If** I do well, I**'ll win** a trip to space camp!

1 The future progressive stresses that an action **is happening now** / **will happen later**.

2 The future progressive stresses that an action happens **once** / **over a period of time**.

3 The future progressive describes a **plan** / **decision**.

C **Look at the program.** Complete the sentences. What will the people be doing at the different times?

1 At 1:25, the principal _____will be reading_____ her opening message.

2 At 1:40, two astronauts _____ about life in space.

3 At 2:20, a NASA engineer _____ how rockets work.

4 At 2:35, five students _____ their science project.

5 At 3:50, Professor Reyes _____ out prizes for the best essays.

6 At 4:10, the principal _____ her closing speech.

—————— *School Science Fair* ——————

1:15–1:30	The principal reads her opening message.
1:30–2:00	Two astronauts talk about life in space.
2:00–2:30	A NASA engineer explains how rockets work.
2:30–3:00	Five students present their science project.
3:00–3:30	BREAK
3:30–4:00	Professor Reyes hands out prizes for the best essays.
4:00–4:15	The principal gives her closing speech.

D 🎧 **12.4 Complete the conversation.** Circle the correct answers. Then listen and check.

Chris: What [1] **are you doing / have you done**?

Lucia: Oh, [2] **I'm practicing / I'll practice** my presentation. It's on the spacecraft *Voyager I*. [3] **I was / I've been** interested in it since I was in elementary school.

Chris: Hmm. I don't know anything about it.

Lucia: Well, NASA [4] **launched / is launching** it in 1977. It [5] **traveled / has traveled** through our solar system until 2012.

Chris: Why did it stop? What [6] **happened / has happened** in 2012?

Lucia: It didn't stop. It [7] **is leaving / left** our solar system. It's still out there, and [8] **it's carrying / it will carry** all kinds of things, like recordings of languages, music, and photos. If aliens [9] **find / will find** it, [10] **they learn / they'll learn** a lot about Earth.

Chris: Wow! That's amazing.

Lucia: Since then, [11] **it continued / it's continued** to travel and send back information to Earth. But scientists think it [12] **has run / will run** out of power someday.

E **Work with a partner. Student A:** Turn to page 151. **Student B:** Turn to page 155. You are going to see how much you know about our solar system.

SPACE INVENTIONS

Astronaut Bruce McCandless II
testing a new space jet pack in 1987

A ▶ 12.1 **Watch the video.** Circle **T** for True or **F** for False.

1 NASA's water filter helped astronauts recycle water in space.   **T**   **F**

2 NASA used its infrared technology to measure distances in space.   **T**   **F**

3 Glass lenses break more often than plastic lenses.   **T**   **F**

4 Lenses made of NASA's new plastic scratched easily.   **T**   **F**

DO YOU KNOW?

What sport have astronauts played on the moon?
a golf
b baseball
c tennis

B ▶ 12.1 **Watch again.** What are some ways the inventions have helped? Match the two parts of the sentences.

1 NASA's new plastic   ○   ○ makes camping easier.

2 NASA's water filter   ○   ○ helps prevent eye injuries.

3 NASA's infrared technology ○   ○ allows hospitals to treat people quickly.

C **Look at the pictures.** NASA helped develop these gadgets. Match the gadgets with the problems NASA needed to solve.

a   b   c   d

NASA needed …

1 _____ to make computers easier to use.

2 _____ small cameras to fit onto their spacecraft.

3 _____ to collect small rocks from the moon to study on Earth.

4 _____ a way for astronauts to communicate from their spacesuits.

D CRITICAL THINKING Evaluating **Talk with a partner.** Which inventions in **B** and **C** do you think are the most useful? Pick three and explain your choices to your partner.

> **PROJECT What problems do astronauts have in space?** Think of an invention to help solve one of their problems. Create a poster for your invention.

PRONUNCIATION linking of /w/ and /y/ sounds

🎧 12.5 **Listen.** Write the sound between the underlined words (w or y). Then listen again and repeat the sentences.

1 Pluto isn't a planet anymore.   _____

2 We can see a lot of stars in the sky.   _____

3 We'll be arriving at noon tomorrow.   _____

4 You only see auroras at night.   _____

COMMUNICATION

Work in groups. Imagine you are going on a trip to the moon. You will be living there for a month. Choose three items below to take with you, and add three items of your own.

books	magazines	movies	music	playing cards
sunglasses	your phone	a board game	a knife	a pen and paper
a soccer ball	a telescope	_____	_____	_____

> I'm bringing my phone to the moon. It has a great camera.

> I'm bringing a soccer ball. We can play soccer in our spacesuits!

READING

A **Read the title.** What do you think an exoplanet is? Read paragraph A to check your answer.

   a an extremely large planet

   b a planet outside our solar system

   c a planet that contains life

B **Scan the text.** Underline the words that go with these definitions.

   a a tool you use to see faraway objects (paragraph A)

   b devices that produce powerful beams of light (paragraph D)

C **Predict.** Look at the picture below. What features do you think make this planet Earthlike?

EXOPLANETS

A 🎧 **12.6** For a long time, scientists could only imagine what planets outside our solar system were like. Now, they are able to see them. Telescope technology has improved **significantly**, and in the past 30 years, scientists have **located** over 4,000 exoplanets. And they are finding new ones every week.

Shapes and Sizes

B There are many types of exoplanets. Some are so hot that any water on them has boiled away. Others are so cold that they are **forever** frozen in ice. Some worlds have fallen into their stars. And others have been thrown out of their solar systems. One planet orbits its star so quickly that a year there is less than three days on Earth!

C However, a few of these worlds are similar to ours. Like Earth, they have a rocky **surface** and liquid water. Scientists are especially interested in these planets. They believe that the easiest way to find them is to look near stars that are smaller and less bright than our own sun. By searching around these stars, scientists have found about 50 Earthlike planets, including Gliese 581d—the "super Earth."

Signs of Life

D But what's next after finding an Earthlike planet? Some scientists look for something never before seen outside of Earth: life. They look for gases like oxygen and methane, or for something called the "red edge." This is the red light that a planet full of green plants **reflects**. They also search for the "techno-signatures" an advanced species might produce, like lights, lasers, and forms of pollution. Scientists even look for large **objects** built around stars to collect their energy.

Endless Possibilities

E Our search for exoplanets is an exciting one. In a few years, NASA will be launching its newest and most powerful telescope into space. What new things will we discover? Will we find a second home for humans? Or will we learn something else—that we aren't alone in the universe? Only time will tell.

An Earthlike planet orbits the star Gliese 581.

COMPREHENSION

IDIOM

If you lose focus and stop paying attention, you _____ .
a moon out
b space out
c star out

A **Answer the questions about *Exoplanets*.**

1 MAIN IDEA Choose another title for this article.

   a Alone in the Universe

   b Traveling to the Stars

   c Other Earths

2 DETAIL Which of these statements is NOT true about exoplanets?

   a Most exoplanets are not like Earth.

   b Exoplanets are becoming easier to find.

   c Exoplanets usually have a rocky surface and liquid water.

3 PURPOSE The main purpose of paragraph C is to _____ .

   a explain the importance of Gliese 581d

   b describe how scientists find Earthlike planets

   c show that exoplanets are mainly found near small stars

4 DETAIL Scientists locate Earthlike planets by _____ .

   a looking for red edges

   b searching for techno-signatures

   c searching the area around particular stars

5 INFERENCE Which discovery on an exoplanet would probably excite scientists most?

   a a liquid surface   b oxygen   c forms of pollution

B **Categorize the things scientists are searching for.** Are they natural or are they examples of techno-signatures? Write the letters (**a**–**g**) in the correct column.

a a red edge
b a rocky surface
c large objects around stars
d lights and lasers
e liquid water
f oxygen and methane
g pollution

Natural	Techno-signatures

C CRITICAL THINKING Evaluating **Talk with a partner.** Do you think scientists will discover life on another planet? Why or why not?

VOCABULARY

A **Find the words below in the article.** Then complete the passage. Use the correct form of the words in the box.

significantly	locate	forever	surface	reflect	object

It's the brightest [1] _____ in our night sky. The moon is almost 400,000 kilometers away, but it affects the Earth [2] _____. It moves the oceans, and it helps keep our planet turning steadily. Despite its brightness, it doesn't create any light of its own. Instead, it [3] _____ light from the sun. It has a dry and rocky [4] _____ that is very dusty. And using telescopes, astronomers have [5] _____ many craters on it—giant holes created by space objects that hit it. The moon formed 4.5 billion years ago, and it will continue to orbit Earth [6] _____.

B **Read the information.** Then add *-like* to the words in the box to complete the sentences below.

> We can add the suffix *-like* to certain words to say something is similar to it.
>
> *They found an Earthlike planet. = They found a planet that is similar to Earth.*

cat	child	dream	Earth	life

1 She'll be making a realistic and _____ statue of that soldier.

2 When he talks about space, his excitement is almost _____.

3 The movie he's making has a strange _____ quality to it.

4 Scientists are looking for _____ planets outside our solar system.

5 The dancer's movements were quick, graceful, and almost _____.

WRITING

A **Read the passage.** Do you agree or disagree?

B **Is space exploration important?** Why or why not? Make notes.

C **Write a paragraph.** State your opinion and give reasons.

I believe that space exploration is very important. When we explore, we learn new things about the universe and ourselves. Scientists have discovered many things because of space exploration. If we don't continue exploring space, ...

THE **RED** PLANET

Before You Watch

Take a quiz. Work with a partner. Circle **T** for True or **F** for False. What else do you know about Mars?

1   It is the closest planet to Earth.   **T**   **F**

2   You can see Mars from Earth without a telescope.   **T**   **F**

3   Mars's atmosphere is mostly carbon dioxide.   **T**   **F**

While You Watch

A ▶ 12.2 **Watch the video.** Circle the correct answers.

1   Mars is the **second** / **fourth** smallest planet in our solar system.

2   Mars used to be much **cooler** / **warmer** billions of years ago.

3   We know that Mars once **had lakes** / **supported life**.

4   Mars's volcanoes are **still active** / **now extinct**.

B ▶ 12.2 **Watch again.** Complete the sentences. Use the correct words from the box. Two words are extra.

ice	life	rivers	surface	volcanoes	war

1   To the ancient Romans, Mars was the god of _____ .

2   Mars has many _____ , like Olympus Mons.

3   Today, you can find _____ at Mars's poles.

4   Some scientists think there was once _____ on Mars.

C   **Some scientists believe we will be able to live on Mars in the future.** Check (✓) three possible reasons.

☐ It is smaller than Earth.   ☐ It has a solid surface.

☐ It is cold.   ☐ It has high mountains.

☐ It has ice at its poles.   ☐ It is close enough to travel to.

After You Watch

Talk with a partner. What do we have to change about Mars to make it habitable?

NASA's Curiosity rover on the surface of Mars

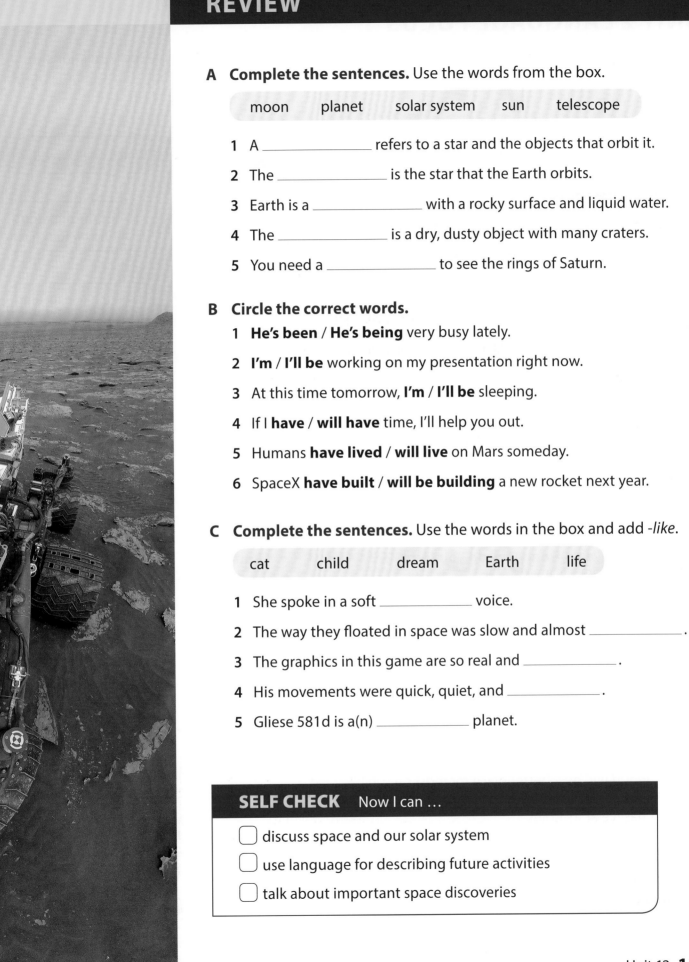

REVIEW

A Complete the sentences. Use the words from the box.

| moon | planet | solar system | sun | telescope |

1 A _____ refers to a star and the objects that orbit it.

2 The _____ is the star that the Earth orbits.

3 Earth is a _____ with a rocky surface and liquid water.

4 The _____ is a dry, dusty object with many craters.

5 You need a _____ to see the rings of Saturn.

B Circle the correct words.

1 **He's been / He's being** very busy lately.

2 **I'm / I'll be** working on my presentation right now.

3 At this time tomorrow, **I'm / I'll be** sleeping.

4 If I **have / will have** time, I'll help you out.

5 Humans **have lived / will live** on Mars someday.

6 SpaceX **have built / will be building** a new rocket next year.

C Complete the sentences. Use the words in the box and add *-like*.

| cat | child | dream | Earth | life |

1 She spoke in a soft _____ voice.

2 The way they floated in space was slow and almost _____.

3 The graphics in this game are so real and _____.

4 His movements were quick, quiet, and _____.

5 Gliese 581d is a(n) _____ planet.

SELF CHECK   Now I can ...

☐ discuss space and our solar system

☐ use language for describing future activities

☐ talk about important space discoveries

UNIT 2 LANGUAGE FOCUS

Student A: Look at the picture below. The girls' names are missing. Ask your partner questions to identify the girls.

Wendy   Tina   Beth   Grace   Delia

UNIT 6 LANGUAGE FOCUS

A Work with a partner. Take turns asking and answering the survey questions. Mark your own responses and your partner's responses.

1 = definitely not   2 = probably not   3 = probably   4 = definitely

50 years from now, do you think … ?	You	Your partner
people will live longer		
more people will have enough food		
scientists will find a cure for cancer		
we will end climate change		
there will be less pollution		
food will become cheaper		
new types of energy will become common		
the world will be a better place for most people		

B Add up your scores. Are you optimistic or pessimistic about the future?

0–15	You are pessimistic. You feel that the future is not very bright.
16–23	You are neither positive nor negative about the future.
24–32	You are optimistic. You feel that the future is full of promise.

UNIT 7 COMMUNICATION

Student A: Take turns asking questions. Give the three possible answers. Check (✓) the questions the other two students get correct. The correct answers are in **bold**.

	Student B	Student C
1 When did color TVs start appearing in people's homes? a in the 1930s **b in the 1950s** c in the 1970s	☐	☐
2 How long was Neil Armstrong on the surface of the moon? **a for 21 hours** b for 41 hours c for 3 days	☐	☐
3 When did Albert Einstein live? a from 1849 to 1925 b from 1864 to 1940 **c from 1879 to 1955**	☐	☐
4 When did the dodo bird go extinct? a about 100 years ago **b about 300 years ago** c about 1,000 years ago	☐	☐
5 When did the United States become independent? a on October 12, 1492 b on January 1,1608 **c on July 4, 1776**	☐	☐

UNIT 12 LANGUAGE FOCUS

Student A: Take turns asking questions. Give the two possible answers. Check (✓) the questions your partner gets correct. The correct answers are in **bold**.

	Student B
1 After the moon, what's the brightest object in the night sky? **a Venus** b Mars	☐
2 What is the moon slowly doing? a moving toward Earth **b moving away from Earth**	☐
3 Where is the highest volcano in the solar system? a on Earth **b on Mars**	☐
4 How many astronauts have walked on the moon? a 3 **b 12**	☐
5 If you fly a spacecraft between Mars and Jupiter, what will you see? **a an asteroid belt** b a human-made satellite	☐

UNIT 2 LANGUAGE FOCUS

Student B: Look at the picture below. The boys' names are missing. Ask your partner questions to identify the boys.

Sam   Ricardo   Kevin   Josh   Tom

UNIT 9 LANGUAGE FOCUS

Student A: Look at this picture of Rick from twenty years ago. Your partner has a picture of Rick today. Ask and answer questions to find out what's different. Find at least five differences.

UNIT 7 COMMUNICATION

Student B: Take turns asking questions. Give the three possible answers. Check (✓) the questions the other two students get correct. The correct answers are in **bold**.

	Student A	Student C
1 When did Facebook first appear online? a in 1998 **b in 2004** c in 2008	☐	☐
2 How long did the first journey around the world last? a 1 year **b 3 years** c 5 years	☐	☐
3 When did Leonardo da Vinci paint the *Mona Lisa*? **a in the 1500s** b in the 1600s c in the 1700s	☐	☐
4 When did the Spanish artist Pablo Picasso live? a from 1781 to 1873 b from 1831 to 1923 **c from 1881 to 1973**	☐	☐
5 When was William Shakespeare born? **a about 460 years ago** b about 310 years ago c about 150 years ago	☐	☐

UNIT 10 LANGUAGE FOCUS

Student A: Ask your partner questions to complete the passage. You and Student B have the same passage, but with different parts missing. Write the questions you need to ask. Then take turns asking and answering the questions. Write the missing information.

Dawn Tyson has lived [1] _____ for over 50 years. She has had a quiet life. She got married when [3] _____ . Since then, she has worked at a supermarket. On the night of August 4, she heard [5] _____ outside. She went out to investigate. She saw a large hole in her backyard. A large reddish rock was inside it. She called [7] _____ . They showed the rock to scientists, who said that the rock was a meteorite! Meteorites are worth a lot of money. The local museum paid Dawn $75,000 for the rock.

1 Where _____ ?

3 When _____ ?

5 What _____ ?

7 Who _____ ?

UNIT 7 COMMUNICATION

Student C: Take turns asking questions. Give the three possible answers. Check (✓) the questions the other two students get correct. The correct answers are in **bold**.

			Student A	Student B
1 How long did the first flight in an airplane last? **a for 12 seconds** **b** for 32 seconds **c** for 52 seconds			☐	☐
2 When did Mahatma Gandhi live? **a** from 1849 to 1928 **b from 1869 to 1948** **c** from 1909 to 1968			☐	☐
3 When did Apple release the first iPad? **a** in 2003 **b** in 2007 **c in 2010**			☐	☐
4 When did hip hop music begin? **a in the 1970s** **b** in the 1990s **c** in the 2010s			☐	☐
5 When did Confucius live? **a** 1,500 years ago **b 2,500 years ago** **c** 3,500 years ago			☐	☐

UNIT 9 LANGUAGE FOCUS

Student B: Look at this picture of Rick today. Your partner has a picture of Rick from twenty years ago. Ask and answer questions to find out what's different. Find at least five differences.

Rick used to have long hair. Does he still have long hair?

No, now he has short hair. Did he use to have a tablet?

UNIT 10 LANGUAGE FOCUS

Student B: Ask your partner questions to complete the passage. You and Student A have the same passage, but with different parts missing. Write the questions you need to ask. Then take turns asking and answering the questions. Write the missing information.

Dawn Tyson has lived in Dayton for over 50 years. She has had a ^{2}_____ life. She got married when she was 24. Since then, she has worked at ^{4}_____. On the night of August 4, she heard a loud noise outside. She went out to investigate. She saw ^{6}_____ in her backyard. A large reddish rock was inside it. She called the police. They showed the rock to ^{8}_____, who said that the rock was a meteorite! Meteorites are worth a lot of money. The local museum paid Dawn $75,000 for the rock.

2 What kind of _____?

4 Where _____?

6 What _____?

8 Who _____?

UNIT 12 LANGUAGE FOCUS

Student B: Take turns asking questions. Give the two possible answers. Check (✓) the questions your partner gets correct. The correct answers are in **bold**.

	Student A
1 Which planet is the closest in size to Earth? a Mars **b Venus**	☐
2 How many moons does Jupiter have? a 9 **b 79**	☐
3 How long does light take to travel from the Sun to Earth? a 10 seconds **b 10 minutes**	☐
4 How long have human-made satellites been in space? **a since the 1950s** b since the 1970s	☐
5 What will the Sun eventually become? a a black hole **b a white dwarf**	☐

IRREGULAR PAST TENSE VERBS

Base form	Past form	Past participle
become	became	become
bring	brought	brought
buy	bought	bought
catch	caught	caught
choose	chose	chosen
come	came	come
cost	cost	cost
cut	cut	cut
draw	drew	drawn
drink	drank	drunk
drive	drove	driven
eat	ate	eaten
fall	fell	fallen
feel	felt	felt
fight	fought	fought
find	found	found
fly	flew	flown
get	got	gotten
give	gave	given
go	went	gone
grow	grew	grown
hear	heard	heard
hurt	hurt	hurt
keep	kept	kept
know	knew	known
let	let	let
lose	lost	lost

Base form	Past form	Past participle
make	made	made
mean	meant	meant
meet	met	met
pay	paid	paid
put	put	put
read	read	read
ride	rode	ridden
run	ran	run
say	said	said
see	saw	seen
sell	sold	sold
show	showed	shown
sing	sang	sung
sink	sank	sunk
sleep	slept	slept
speak	spoke	spoken
steal	stole	stolen
swim	swam	swum
take	took	taken
teach	taught	taught
tell	told	told
think	thought	thought
throw	threw	thrown
understand	understood	understood
wear	wore	worn
win	won	won
write	wrote	written